ISBN 978-1-330-53605-6
PIBN 10075291

1 MONTH OF
FREE
READING

at
www.ForgottenBooks.com

By purchasing this book you are eligible for one month membership to ForgottenBooks.com, giving you unlimited access to our entire collection of over 700,000 titles via our web site and mobile apps.

To claim your free month visit:

www.forgottenbooks.com/free75291

THE DEAD
HAVE NEVER DIED

THE DEAD
HAVE NEVER DIED
EDWARD C. RANDALL

New York · Alfred A. Knopf 1917

"*I tell you with all the strength and conviction I can utter that we do persist, that people over there still take an interest in what is going on here; that they still help us and know far more about things than we do, and are able from time to time to communicate with us.*"

Sir Oliver Lodge.

FOREWORD

I have had strange experiences in my Psychic investigations during the last twenty years. Refusing to be limited by accepted laws, I have devoted my thought to conditions prevailing beyond what is generally termed the material, and by combining and blending the mental and vital, with the tangible or physical forces, I have been able to have speech with those long thought dead. As a result I have found an unknown country about and beyond this Earth, and I would not go from this world of men without leaving a record of what I have learned. We are but custodians of knowledge as of wealth, and it is the duty of every one to give to others that which he has acquired, whenever it will add to human happiness.

There are certain people born with what is known as "psychic" force who, when scientifically developed, become instruments by the aid of which communication is established between the two worlds. Such was Emily S. French. She was a woman over 80 years of age at the time of her death. Above the average in intelligence, she devoted her life to helping others, and as a result her character was spiritualized and refined so that only good could come within her environment. I was indeed fortunate in my association with her. Even with such help, however, it required many years of work and experiment to obtain the exact conditions whereby satisfactory speech could be had with inhabitants of this unknown country, and from them to secure direct information of the conditions prevailing there. This, in a measure, I have accomplished.

That life continues beyond the grave, Lombroso, Richet, Sir William Crookes, T. W. Stanford, William T. Stead, Sir Oliver Lodge,—all Psychic Scientists,—and of late Sir Conan Doyle, have proved beyond question. My efforts have been to discover by what law survival becomes possible; to learn something of the death change, the character of individual life as it continues, and the conditions prevailing beyond the earth-plane. If the information that I have obtained is reliable, and if my deductions are correct, a discovery has been made that takes from the human heart the awful fear of death. No subject in the world is so important as this, and none is less understood.

In this world-beyond there are men and women just as here. Their bodies, Etheric in character, are composed of matter; therefore, they have form, feature, and expression, neither less nor more individual than when they lived the earth-life. They have homes as tangible to them as our homes are to us, composed of Etheric material just as our homes are made of physical substances, and in those homes the family relation is ultimately continued. They labour to increase their knowledge, and under the great prevailing law in force there, enrich themselves by helping others.

These propositions, far beyond human experiences, are not only hard to explain but are difficult to grasp. In the chapters that follow, I have tried to make the facts so plain that all may comprehend them. I have faithfully described some of my experiences, and given in substance the data as presented to me. Are my deductions warranted?

This research has been a source of great pleasure and profit to me. In the beginning I looked upon the death change with horror. I recall the casket containing the mortal remains of my mother lowered into a grave on a bleak April day, the pitiless rain, the biting winds, the lowering clouds. After the frozen earth had fallen into the open grave, I, a boy, walked alone, and then and there resolved that I would never rest content until I had solved the problem there presented and come to know,—if it was given man to learn,—something of that great change. Whether I have succeeded or not you must judge. I have, I think, demonstrated that nothing in Nature is hidden from man; there is no problem that cannot be solved; there is no condition that cannot be understood, provided that we labour long and earnestly for the goal desired.

Again one word to those who mourn. There is no death; there are no dead. Those whom we love and who loved us, in obedience to the great law of evolution, have simply progressed to a new plane of existence. Our eyes no longer behold them, our hands and lips no longer touch them, but their eyes behold and their hands touch us, though we feel them not. They walk with us, know our trials, help us by their mental suggestions, and comfort us by tender, loving thoughts. Those who live in the Etheric or Mental Plane are no less real to me than those with whom I walk from day to day.

I have submitted this manuscript to a large number of advanced thinkers both in America and in Europe, and the general criticism has been that it is so in advance of experience, so different from the old teachings and beliefs, that few will grasp or understand the new propositions presented. This is without doubt true, but the facts as I have gathered them cannot be changed; truth is infinite.

Volumes have been written by the world's foremost writers to prove the possibility of communication between this plane and the next, though few have been privileged to enjoy direct and independent speech to the extent that I have. Those who read the pages that I have written must assume that speech is possible and that I have had the experiences narrated. I do not attempt to enter the elementary field; others have covered that branch. I have tried to transmit facts as they have been given me, and I expect many to accept them because they are in accordance with nature's law and appeal to reason.

It is a great privilege to be evolved out of the mass of life, to obtain individuality with all its possibilities not by a miracle, but through positive law. But that privilege brings responsibilities, among them the necessity of living a clean life, of developing character to the utmost, of doing something to make others happy, and of making the world a little better because we have lived a day within its confines. These things are not difficult to accomplish if we are unselfish. To the new thought, to the progress of the world, each may give something. Great truths come from the obscure. The night brings forth the stars.

EDWARD C. RANDALL.

CONTENTS

Chapter 1   Voices of the Living Dead 15

Chapter 2   A Conscious Dissolution 23

Chapter 3   Speech with the Dead 34

Chapter 4   Told in the After-Life 44

Chapter 5   The Life Mass 53

Chapter 6   The Continuity of Life 63

Chapter 7   A Universe of Matter 76

Chapter 8   The Record of a Night 86

Chapter 9   Atomic Life 97

Chapter 10   Etheric Environment 105

Chapter 11   So Little Change 116

Chapter 12   Man's Etheric Body 126

Chapter 13   The Unknown Land 133

Chapter 14   Personal Identity 140

Chapter 15   Spheres in the After-Life 149

Chapter 16   Their Daily Life 159

Chapter 17   Facts Well to Know 170

Chapter 18   From Death's Sleep 181

Chapter 19   The Imagination 194

CONTENTS

Chapter 20 Power of Suggestion 206

Chapter 21 Never a Secret in the World 215

Chapter 22 Mental Activity 223

Chapter 23 Picture of a Child 233

Chapter 24 Actualities of the After-Life 245

Chapter 25 Rational Deductions 251

Chapter 26 A Tribute 258

THE DEAD HAVE NEVER DIED

CHAPTER I

VOICES OF THE LIVING DEAD

THE suggestion that the dead have never died, when so little is known of that great change, is beyond the comprehension of the average mind. The fact that under scientific conditions those in the after-life have had speech with us in the earth-life taxes credulity, but such is the fact. Sir William Crookes has had the experience of communicating with the dead and has written concerning it. Stead's bureau in London, working with Mrs. Weidt, an American psychic, has done so with great freedom. For many years Daniel Bailey of Buffalo was able with the aid of Mrs. Swaine to get the direct or independent voice; he did a great work and has published the results.

I mention these instances to show that I am not the first who has been able to obtain direct speech with those in the next life. Thousands in other ways have obtained messages from the great beyond, but only on rare occasions have conditions been such that the dead could speak audibly. The independent voice is unusual, but when heard, it leaves nothing to conjecture.

"How is it possible," one asks, "to talk with dead people?"

I confess that such a proposition is beyond the comprehension of many, and that a mere statement on the subject means nothing to the average individual, for one can appreciate only those things which he has experienced or of which he has knowledge. It is only by understanding that the spirit world is a part of this world, that it is here and about us, that it is material, that all life force finds expression only in the physical, and that people beyond the grave still inhabit their etheric bodies that one can appreciate the fact that speech with the living dead is possible. Even with such an understanding, it is necessary to create certain scientific conditions if one would actually converse with those of the spirit world. The conditions permitting speech are very delicate. The atmosphere at times interferes with results. For example, when the air is agitated before a storm, it is impossible to do this work; but on clear nights, when the air is quiet, the manifestations are beyond power of description. Absolute darkness is necessary to enable me to hear the direct speech of those people who, present in my home in their own spirit bodies, use their own tongues, and make their own voice vibrations. To do this work requires the aid of a person possessed of vital forces out of the ordinary. The group of people in the next life working with me utilized the vital force of Mrs. Emily S. French in conjunction with their own force, and created a new condition in which the vibrations were slow. It was then possible for the spirits to so clothe their organs of speech that their words sounded in our atmosphere. If we accept the hypothesis that spirit people have bodies, and that they are around and about us in an invisible world, it does not require any stretch of imagination to appreciate the possibility of speaking with those beyond the earth-plane. When we appreciate the fundamental fact that the Universe is matter and that life itself is matter, new possibilities open to us.

"Tell us of the conditions that enable you to speak," I asked one who spoke to us.

"There are in our group," the spirit replied,

"seven people,—all expert in the handling of the electric and magnetic forces, and when you and the psychic, Mrs. French, meet, the vital force that emanates from her personality is gathered up.   We also take physical emanations—substances—from you and the others with you, while we contribute to the mass a certain spirit force.   Now, that force which we gather and distribute, is just as material as any substance that you would gather for any purpose; it is simply higher in vibration.   We clothe the organs of respiration of the spirit who is to speak, so that his voice will sound in your atmosphere, and when this condition is brought about, it is just as natural for a spirit as it is for you. You then have what is known as the direct or independent voice, that is, the voice of a spirit speaking as in earth-life."

Since mankind came up out of savagery, the great problem has been and ever will be: What is the ultimate end?   What, if anything, waits on the other side of death's mysterious door?   What happens when the hour strikes that closes man's earth career, when, leaving all the gathered wealth of lands and goods, he goes out into the dark alone? Is death the end—annihilation and repose?   Or, does he awake in some other sphere or condition, retaining individuality and identity?

Each must solve this great question for himself. Dissolution and change have come to every form of life, and will come to all that live. With opportunity knocking at the door, mankind has but little more appreciation of it now than it had when Phallic-worship swayed the destinies of empires. It may be that, as a people, our development has been such that we could heretofore grasp and comprehend only length, breadth, and thickness, the three accepted dimensions of matter; that in our progression we have but now become able to appreciate and understand life forces that find their expression beyond the physical plane.

Time was when all knowledge was handed down from one generation to another by story, song, and tradition. When the Persian civilization was growing old, and ambition towered above the lofty walls of Babylon; when Egypt was building her temples on the banks of the Nile; when Greece was the centre of art and culture, and Rome with its wealth and luxuries held sway over the civilized world, people did not dream of type and the printing press, applied electricity, or navigation of the air, and the many inventions that were to come. They were not ready for such progression.

The world cannot stand still. The great law of the universe is progress. Two or three generations since, the idea that a cable would one day be laid under the sea and that messages would be transmitted under the waters and over the waters from continent to continent, was laughed at as a chimera. Only a little while ago, the world could not understand how words and sentences could be flashed across the trackless ocean from ship to ship, and from land to land, without wires, in space. And who shall now say that it is not possible to send thoughts, words, sentences, voices even, and messages, out into the ether of the spirit world, there to be heard, recorded, and answered? Has man reached the end of his possibilities; will all progression stop with Marconi's achievements and telephoning without wires? This is the age of man; we have passed the age of gods. If our development is such that we can comprehend the life and conditions following dissolution, it must be within our grasp as surely as progress has been possible at all times and among all people since the world began.

Our age is one of sudden and rapid changes. What was true yesterday assumes a different, one could almost say, a diametrically opposite aspect to-day. Our people are in a state of transition. New views come with changing times and conditions. Most minds are sensitive, alert, and versatile, and the present is fraught with unrest and a thirst for knowledge. This is a period that will be fruitful in scientific discoveries, and in the adaptation of the universal law of vibratory action. We need not be afraid of investigation. All truth is safe; nothing else will suffice, and he who holds back the truth, through expediency or fear, fails in his duty to mankind.

Some have come to know what awaits over the great divide, have solved the great problem of dissolution, and with the confidence born of knowledge, based on facts proved and demonstrated, are ready to speak with authority. As one among the many, I again give the world the result of my continued research in the new field of psychic science.

We have looked upon the discarded physical body, habitation or housing, occupied by one while developing on the earth plane, and have said: "He is dead; never again will his voice speak words of tenderness, his hands touch, or eyes look upon us, nevermore will we know his tender loving care; he is no more" Such is the most erroneous conclusion ever reached by the human mind. When at night we lay aside our clothing, we are the same. When at the end of a short span we separate from the flesh garment we have worn, we are not dead. We are identically the same person, mentally, morally, and spiritually as before, with the same etheric body, with power to think and function as in earth-life. I say with all the strength and force at my command that there is continuity of all life; that nothing is ever lost; that communication is possible, and has been had with those in the after-life in many ways. My effort has been to create a condition in which it became possible for spirit people to clothe with physical substance their organs of respiration, so they could talk to us as when in earth-life. It has been my privilege to hear their voices, best of all methods, hundreds of times. Thousands of individuals have spoken, using their own vocal organs, and I have answered. From this source has come great knowledge, facts beyond the learning of men, not found in any books, and it is my privilege to give them to you.

Lay aside preconceived notions, discard prejudice, be fair and unafraid, while in simple language, I relate what has come to me from this wonderful source. If you are not impressed with its truth, discard it. If it appeals to reason, it will be a help not only here but hereafter.

CHAPTER II

YES, I know that I am no longer an inhabitant of the earth sphere, that I am numbered among the dead; so because I thoroughly understand the great change through which I have passed, the group of spirit people working with you, and controlling conditions on this side, have asked me to speak to you, and through you to all those who sorrow for their dead. You know, of course, that in speaking I am now using my own voice."

Out of the silence, out of the darkness, in a room devoted solely to psychic investigation came those words; one whom the world calls dead was speaking. I have never ceased to be startled when a voice first speaks from the invisible world—so unusual, so marvellous, so wonderful, and yet to me so natural. I know of but two psychics who are able to contribute to conditions that make the direct or independent voice possible. Emily S. French, who devoted to my work the best years of her life, was one of them, and on this occasion she

23

was alone with me in the room in my own home devoted solely to such work.   At this time the conditions were such that it was possible for those out of the earth body to so talk that their voices were audible.

The public wants to know, and I had always wanted to know, the sensation involved in the death change, in the awakening; what it is that the eyes behold, or the ears hear when first consciousness continues or returns.   So when this man spoke so clearly and strongly, I determined to get from one who had made the change a comprehensive statement of the mental state, not only before but after the transition.

"So much," I said, "of the information that we get from the plane where you now live is general in character, won't you be specially specific and tell us, first, something of your occupation and of the conditions immediately preceding your dissolution?"

"I came," he replied, "from a long line of soldiers.   My ancestors fought in the American Revolution, and were among those who aided in establishing your Republic; possibly I inherited a martial spirit.   When the first shot was fired by the Confederates, and Lincoln issued his call for volunteers, I was possessed with a desire to enter the army. I had a wife and two children, to whom as I now know, I owed a far greater duty than to my country, but the speech of people, the danger of the nation, the condition of slavery prevailing in the Southern States, and the preparation for war, incited me. With forced words of good cheer, I left the brave wife and little children, enlisted, and became a soldier of the Union.

"I will not take the time to tell you of my life in the army, except to speak of the nights in camp when my thoughts went out to those at home, knowing as I did that funds were slowly diminishing. Ever the idea was dominant that the war would soon be over, then there would be the home coming, and the plans I formed to make compensation for my long absence would come to fruition. But the war did not end as battle after battle was fought with success first on one side, then on the other. I participated in many, seeming to bear a charmed life, for while thousands about me fell, I passed unharmed, and so grew fearless."

"Under what circumstances did you meet your end," I asked.

"It was at Gettysburg," he replied, "I can see and feel it all again as my mind concentrates on that tragic event. It was the second day of that great fight. I was then a colonel and commanded a regiment in reserve; in front of us the battle roared. Shot and shell filled the air and fell near us, muskets belched forth their fire, the earth seemed to tremble; wounded in great numbers were carried to the rear, and we knew that countless dead lay where they had fallen. We waited, knowing it was only a matter of hours, possibly minutes before the order would come to advance. I looked down the line at blanched faces, we all knew that many would not answer the roll call at night. Still we waited. Suddenly out of the smoke galloped an officer from the general's staff. 'Forward,' came the command.

"There was no faltering now that the hour had come. The column moved. Soon shot and shell fell among us, on we went. All was excitement, fear was gone; we had but one desire, and that to kill; such is the lust of battle. I recall but little more. We reached the front and saw the grey line charging up the hill toward us; then, oblivion. I now know that I was shot."

"Tell me of returning consciousness and what you saw," I said.

"You must remember," the spirit answered, "that these tragic events occurred nearly half a century ago, and that at that time it had not been discovered that there is another life, a plane as ma-

terial as the one you now inhabit, where life continues. I had no conception of a hereafter, for
with all my religious teaching I had no idea of what
or where the future life might be; nor was I at all
sure there was one; so you can imagine how startled
I was to awake as from a deep sleep; bewildered I
got to my feet, and looking down saw my body
among many others upon the ground. This was
startling. I made a great effort to collect my
thoughts and recall events. Then I remembered
the awful battle; still I did not then realize I had
been shot. I was apart from, still I seemed in
some way, held to the body I had so lately worn.
My mental condition was one of terrible unrest.
How was it I was alive, had a body and yet separate and apart from the covering I had thought
constituted the body.

"I tried to think and realize my situation. I
looked about; others of the seeming dead moved,
seemed to stir. Then many of them stood up, and
like me seemed to emerge from their physical
bodies, for their old forms still lay upon the field.
I looked at other prostrate bodies, examined many;
from each something was gone. Going among them
again, I found other bodies inhabited, still living
as you would say, though wounded and unconscious.

"Soon I found myself among thousands in a similar mental state. Not one among them knew just what had happened. I did not know then as I do now, that I always possessed a spirit body composed of a material called Ether, and that the physical body was only the garment it wore while in earth life."

"What brought you to the full realization of what had happened?" I asked.

"I am coming to that," he said; "While the passing out of the old body was without pain, it is a terrible thing to drive a strong spirit from a healthy body, tear it from its coverings. It is unnatural, and the sensation following readjustment is awful. In a short time I became easier, but I was still bewildered. It was neither night nor day; about us all was gloom, not a ray of light, nor a star. Something like an atmosphere dark and red enveloped us all, and we waited in fear and silence; we seemed to feel one another's thoughts, or to be more correct, hear one another think. No words were spoken. How long we remained in this state I cannot now tell, for we do not measure time as you do. Soon there was a ray of light that grew brighter each moment, and then a great concourse of men and women with kindly faces came, and with comforting words told us not to fear; that we had made the great change; that death so-called only advanced our sphere of life; that we were still living beings, inhabitants now of the first plane beyond the earth; that we would live on forever, and by labour reach a higher mental development; that for us the war was over, we had passed through the valley of death.

"I will not attempt to tell you of the sorrow that came with such realization, not for myself, for I soon learned that only through death could we progress, and that the personal advantages beyond the physical were greater than those in the physical; it was sorrow for the wife and the babies; their great grief when they learned what had happened, bound me to their condition, and we sorrowed together. I could not progress or find happiness until time had healed their sorrow. If only those in earth life knew that their sadness binds and holds us, stays our progress and development! After coming with the aid of many friends to full consciousness, and being able to move at will, I followed at first the movements of both armies. I saw the route of Lee's army, the final surrender at Appomattox, and I want to tell you of the great effort the inhabitants of this land in which I live put forth, not only to prevent war, but to bring peace when nations or people are at war, for war

has never been right. No taking of human life
is ever justifiable.

"This is the first time it has been my personal
privilege to get a message through to the world
I once inhabited. It has been a great pleasure to
tell you something of the sensations during and
after the change. There is one experience that I
want to relate, for it made a profound impression.
One day I saw many people passing into a building having the appearance of a great Temple of
Music. I was told I could go in if I desired—I
did. There were assembled, I should judge, five
thousand people. They sat with bowed heads in a
silence, so absolute that I marvelled; turning I
asked one beside me the object of the meeting, and
I was told they were concentrating their thoughts,
sending out peace vibrations to nations at war. I
did not comprehend, but, curious, I waited. Soon
above that great company arose a golden cloud that
formed and moved as if directed. Having learned
that I could go at will, I followed and found the
cloudy substance enveloping another battle field.
Again a dark condition with flashes of red, immediately surrounding and above two great armies,
for the thoughts of those in battle give out emanations producing such effect. It had substantially
the same appearance that prevailed on my awaken-

ing. As I watched, the dark condition seemed to change, to dissolve before the peaceful conditions of the light that I had followed, just as mist dissolves before the sun. With the change a better thought filled the minds of those engaged, an inclination to treat more humanly the wounded and the prisoners. This is one of the ways those experienced among us help the mental, as those among you aid the physical; both are equally real.

"Among us are the great who counsel together and work to influence those in authority against war, while others among us by thought suggestions help and sustain those poor soldiers forced into battle, either to satisfy the greed, selfishness, and ambition of those in authority, or to defend a nation or the integrity of their country. We know neither the one side nor the other. We see only the suffering of humanity, a mother's mourning, a wife's heart breaking, a child's sobbing. They are all human, and without distinction or class we labour to comfort and help them by mental suggestion. In such work we enter their homes, a great invisible host, and many a heart has been cheered through our ministrations. Other wars will come, unless the thought of those now in authority changes; then a great work will be required of us, for which we are ready."

"This has been exceedingly interesting, but just one word more. How does your earth-life appear, after so many years?" I asked.

"How much do you remember of those first years, when as an infant you gazed upon your world?" the man replied. "So it is with me. I have but an indistinct recollection of the events that made up my earth-life, only a memory remains, still enough to make me regret many lost opportunities. I was not then a thinker, only a drifter; I accepted what was told me without question; the result was that I did not develop my mental faculties. This life offers such splendid advantages, my joy of living in the present is so intense, that I seldom think of the earth-life at all. All the trials, sorrows, and sufferings incident to birth and the few years in your physical world, were necessary, and from my present vantage ground the matter of living a few years more or less, the manner of my going were unimportant; it is all forgotten now in the wonderful reality about me. As soon as I came to understand what death was and to what it led, I immediately commenced to complete my education, and build a home for the wife and children, and I am happy to tell you that again we dwell together, for they are all here in this land of happiness and opportunity."

In the presence of such an experience, listening to an individual speaking from the world beyond, telling of another, an unknown land, where all the so-called dead live, think, move, develop, and progress, the learned should understand and comprehend that three dimensions and five senses do not explain the conditions beyond,

"The Spring blew trumpets of color;
   Her Green sang in my brain.
I saw a blind man groping
   'Tap-tap' with his cane;
I pitied him his blindness;
   But can I boast 'I see'?;
Perhaps there walks a spirit
   Close by, who pities me,—
A spirit who hears me tapping
   The five-sensed cane of the mind,
Amid such unknown glories
   I may be worse than blind."

CHAPTER III

SPEECH WITH THE DEAD

IT was in the year 1892 that I met Emily S. French. She was a woman then over 60 years of age, in delicate health, and very deaf. While she was conscious that she possessed powers out of the ordinary, she had little more comprehension than I of that into which the force would develop. At the suggestion of a number of prominent citizens, I was asked to meet Mrs. French and explain, if I could, the unusual phenomena obtainable.

In one of our early investigations we sat in a dark room, three of us forming a half circle, she facing us. After a time, seeming whispers were faintly heard, and the gentleman sitting with me insisted that he recognized his wife's voice. It was unsatisfactory to me, but I was interested and immediately made an investigation of the character of the psychic. Finding her of good family and of more than ordinary education, I determined to know how the phenomenon was produced. Of course, at that

34

time I could not comprehend the direct voice, nor the possibility of speech with the so-called dead. I was then agnostic. As I look over the situation now, I see that I had neither the experience nor the ability to appreciate the facts, any more than the average reader of this book can comprehend some of the statements made in it. I had to learn, first, that the after-life is etheric, and that people take into the after-life the same spirit body which they had in this life divested of the outer flesh garment. In those days I did not know that we have etheric bodies.

I found in the beginning that Mrs. French stood very much in awe of the play of this pyschic force. One always fears things which he does not understand, and not understanding the unusual phenomena present, she was often very much afraid. I investigated far enough to find that she was possessed of a vital force unknown to me. She was just as much in the dark regarding it as I, and just as much interested. Accordingly she undertook to join me in an investigation, to devote her time without money and without price to the mastery of that force in the hope that good might come. Out of that compact came over twenty years of continued work, and experiences which to me seem worthy of record.

It has been said that we have but five senses. That is to say, the average individual has but five senses developed; some persons, however, have seven. To the five accepted senses I add "psychic sight" and "psychic hearing." Mrs. French possessed both of those. At times she could see people moving in the after-life, not with her physical eye, of course, but by means of psychic sight. She could perceive them so acutely that they were just as real to her as if an impression came upon the retina. This is true, because she could see and describe these·people in the dark just as well as in the light. Again, she had psychic hearing, for I have been able on many occasions in the broad daylight to carry on conversations with persons out of the body (she repeating their words) as satisfactorily as if they were still in their physical bodies, and in such talks I have gone frequently far beyond the knowledge of the psychic.

In the beginning spirit speech was faint from the sphere beyond. I was able to get in touch with only a very ordinary class of spirit people, and I often became impatient that those I most desired did not come. I did not then understand as I now do my own limitations, for now I know that instruction was being given me as fast as I could grasp it. When a new fact was stated, the law and the conditions making such fact possible were explained. The first propositions were very simple, but as the years rolled by, we made great progress. We learned how to form the required environment; there was a whisper and then a voice; then the voice took tone and individuality. In course of time those of the group with whom I was accustomed to have speech were easily recognized.

There was one person in particular with whom from the very first time I worked with Mrs. French I was desirous of talking. This was my mother who left this life in 1873. Time went on, and she did not come. Finally she requested me to meet with Mrs. French under the necessary conditions on May 26, 1896, saying that she would come and go over many things in which we were mutually interested.

About ten o'clock on the appointed morning the Brown Building in Buffalo, then being repaired, collapsed. The street was full of rumors that many people had been killed. The number was put, I think, at six or seven. Of course, there was no way of ascertaining the truth until the debris could be removed and this would require many days.

Mrs. French and I were scarcely seated that

evening when my mother greeted me in her own direct voice, and said with great regret that owing to the accident that morning she must forego the pleasure of our visit until a later time, we could be of great help to those whose lives had been crushed out; they needed assistance. Of course, I readily acquiesced in the suggestion. There was perhaps ten minutes of silence; then a voice, choking and coughing, broke the stillness and cried,—

"My God, the building is falling, the building is falling. This way, this way " The situation was tense and startling. I half rose to my feet. Another voice answered in a strange tongue. The words were not distinguishable, but it seemed to me as if some one was responding to the first call, which was followed in a moment by a woman's voice crying out in great fear, "We will all be killed! Help me, help me."

This was the beginning of what we term our mission work, that is, helping to restore consciousness to those who in leaving the old body are not readily able to regain that condition. There was then, aiding in this work, as I have since learned, a group of seven spirit co-workers who had brought to us these unfortunate people whose spirit-bodies had been crushed out in the fall of this building. We were to restore them to a normal mental condition,

and acting upon the suggestion of the spirit co-
workers I quietly talked with them.   After a time
I told them what had occurred and brought them to
a realization of their situation.   Eventually they
came to understand that in the fall of that building
their spirits had been forced from their physical
bodies, and when they came to realize that in the
catastrophe they had gone out of earth-life, their
sorrow was beyond words.   One told me on that
evening that four people, namely: William P.
Straub, George Metz, Michael Schurzke, a Pole, and
Jennie M. Griffin, a woman, had lost their lives in
the fall of the building.   This was verified some
days later.

After talking with me, voice to voice, they
realized that they had gone through the change
called death.   Then their friends in the after-life
came, were recognized, and took them and gave
them such consolation as was possible under the
unfortunate circumstances.

I asked the leader of the spirit group how it was
that the voices when first heard seemed so strained,
and speech so broken, why there was so much
choking.   He replied that a person, crushed out of
the physical body suddenly, finishes as soon as consciousness and the mental condition are restored,
sentences left unuttered when dissolution came;

that in the awakening he takes on the identical state in which he passed out.

After they had gone Mrs. French said:—

"I see behind you a man probably fifty-five or more years old, strong character I should judge, who has been listening to this conversation. He is looking at you with amazement. He does not seem to understand."

I said to her, "Does he know me?"

She replied, "He answers, 'Yes'."

"Does he give his name?"

"No, not yet."

Of course, being in absolute darkness and not possessing psychic sight or psychic hearing, I could neither see nor hear him, but I asked,

"Did he reside in Buffalo?"

She answered, "No."

I then inquired concerning other localities, and named residents of a city where I had lived for some years, asking,

"Was he a resident of that city?" and Mrs. French replied saying:

"He says that he lived there."

Then I repeated the names of many of my acquaintances, trying to identify the individual who was then present, with an idea that I might have speech with him. Finally Mrs. French said:

"I see the letters H. G. B."

I quickly recalled the individual described and spoke his name. He had been a leading citizen of a neighboring city, a large manufacturer. I recalled many evenings spent at his house with his family, and particularly did I recall his voice. On Sunday evenings he enjoyed the gathering of young people, and at such times there was often singing of popular songs, and many of the old hymns. His voice was unusual, deep, resonant, and he sang very well. It was a voice which, having once been heard, could never be mistaken. He had been out of the body then about five years. After a little time he moved around apparently to the side of Mrs. French, and greeted me. That deep masculine voice would have been recognized if he had not given his name; there was no mistake. He spoke my name as familiarly as he ever did in earth life, and I greeted him as cordially as I ever had in his home.

I had believed that this man had led an exemplary life, for this was the general impression which prevailed in the community where he resided, and I thought he, of all men, would find the best conditions after dissolution. However, he did not yet realize that he had separated from his physical body. He knew some great change had taken place, but he had absolutely no conception of what it was, although five years had elapsed since it occurred. He told me that his wife and children no longer recognized him in his own home, that he spoke to them, that he called to them, that he got on his knees and shrieked their names, but he could not apparently touch them, he could not make them realize his presence; they passed him apathetically. His inability to make himself known in the home where he had always been the dominant personality, the indifference with which he was treated not only by his own family but by others with whom he came in contact, had driven him nearly to desperation. He could not understand the situation at all, and he was fearful that he was verging on insanity, if not completely insane. All was darkness about him, all things were unnatural, and he had become frantic. It was a delicate task to bring this man to a realization of the great change that had taken place, because his present condition was so intensely real. He was the same man, he had the same intellect, the same personality, apparently the same body. Why should he be ignored and overlooked by all whom he had known?

It was only after many explanations that he came to a realizing sense that he had left the physical world of men.   Having in mind the exemplary life which he had led, I told him that I could not understand why he should find himself in such a mental state, and he replied that he had not lived the life for which he had been given credit.

A member of the spirit group present said:

"The wrong done in earth-life binds him to the earth condition.   While he has left his physical body, he has not left the earth and its environment, and having no knowledge of the great beyond to which he has journeyed, he has never progressed beyond the earth plane where he formerly lived, and he cannot comprehend while in that mental state the change that has come to him."

It appeared that he had never left his home, and the narrow environment about it, but in a half awakened, half conscious state had wandered from one to another until by good fortune he had been told that if he would attend upon our work, he would understand the change that had come into his life.   With this unusual experience we said "Good Night" to our group of co-workers, and I walked homeward in deep thought.

What shall be said of our civilization that teaches nothing of the conditions prevailing in the after-life?

CHAPTER IV

TOLD IN THE AFTER-LIFE

IF there is one thing this world ought to know, does not know, and wants to know, it is the process in which and by which an inhabitant of this plane of consciousness leaves the physical body to become an inhabitant of the next or etheric plane. I speak of the earth and the etheric plane, of a here, and a hereafter that I may be understood, but technically this, the next, and all planes of existence are one, differing only in vibratory activity, or modes of motion. The Universe is all a part of one stupendous whole.

Only one who has made the great change, can adequately describe conditions under which people live in the sphere beyond. For many years I have been exchanging with other psychic scientists reports of conditions and lectures from this source. T. W. Stanford of Australia sent me a communication from the after-life received by him, which my group say is a statement of fact, and, therefore, with his permission I quote it as follows:

44

"In my weakness I became unconscious of all around; but soon I became conscious of several things. I realized that something that had held me down and fatally gripped me was gone. I was free, and in the place of weakness and pain and sickness, I had a virility and a vigour which I had never known upon the earth plane. I was also aware that I was in new surroundings, most beautiful. Then I became conscious that I was in the midst of a company of fellow souls, whose voices were filled with happiness, all welcoming me, and others whom I had temporarily lost while upon the earth plane. I then knew that some great change had occurred which had taken from me everything that I had desired to get rid of, or some power, had given to me a delightful experience, which I had often in a measure imagined, but dared scarcely believe that it could be possible.

Surrounded by an innumerable company, I was quite dazzled with the appearance of some who, it was explained to me, were exalted personages. Then there approached one who seemed to be the chief speaker. He said before me was the universe, that time was for me no more, that I was henceforth an inhabitant of a new country. You will ask me—was it all pleasant? Extremely so. How can I illustrate it so that you will understand? Have you ever after taking a long journey become extremely tired and weary, and, at last, at the end of much striving and traveling, come to a house of rest? How you sank down upon

the downy couch. Oh, the delight of it! With
no dreams to disturb your rest, you awoke like a
giant refreshed! To me it was something like
that; although even that is a weak illustration.
But that which brought me greatest happiness was
the knowledge that I had gained what I had once
believed I had lost. I had health, strength, vital-
ity, friends, and relatives restored to me for ever-
more.

I have always been fond of the beautiful. I
have spent days, weeks, and months in the picture
galleries of Europe, looking at the work of the
old masters. Many of them lived hundreds of
years before I came upon the earth plane, and yet
I seemed to have known them all the days of my
life. I have dreamed about them. Da Vinci had
always been my companion, Murillo a choice com-
rade; for Giotto I had a deep, lasting friendship.
I loved the beautiful in all its forms. I loved
Nature—the beautiful lakes of Italy and Switzer-
land, the glorious mountains, the everlasting hills.
My friends in spirit life said to me, "come and see
the House Beautiful." Try and understand, if
you can, that not only are the landscapes spiritual,
but so is the beauty of all that there is on the other
side of life. The physical is only the gross imitation of the spiritual. There is no tongue which
can describe the beauty of the spiritual realms,
wherein are the souls of those who have just entered on their progressive existence—souls who
have striven to do their best according to their

light. I say that there is no tongue that can describe the beauties of that land. Take the best
that you have, and it is poor in comparison. Then
I came next to the spiritual houses, and there I
met with more friends, more relatives, and,
greater, grander still, with those royal souls who
had been my affinities on earth—been companions,
comrades of the brush and palette, and others
whom I had deeply reverenced in my soul.

But I found them much greater, grander, nobler
than they ever were in their earth life, and I was
privileged to be one of their companions. Still I
pressed onward. I came next to a Rest House.
That will sound peculiar. You will say, how can
you have rest houses, if you don't know what it is
to be weary? No, there is no weariness like that
you have experienced on earth; but there are rest
houses, where in the spiritual life we may rest and
have delightful intercourse with our friends. In
the spiritual rest houses, therefore, we entered,
and found there relatives and friends. Some were
not upon the same plane of existence as I was, but
they had been permitted to come down to my sphere
to meet me, so that in effect I could say, "He that
was dead is alive again, he that was lost for a
time is found." And then memory—think of the
joy of memory! I had carried personality and
memory into the spirit world, and I compared the
existence in Rome with that which I was then en-
joying. I tell you that it was the expectancy of
what was still to be which gave me the greatest

pleasure and the greatest joy. There is no joy on earth like that which is in Heaven, for it is un-alloyed.

I became conscious that I had to do something, and that I should have to work, and it was a joy. Could I be a messenger? I thought of some on the earth plane I had loved so dearly, and remembered that they were in spiritual darkness. I inquired,— Where is the Heaven of orthodoxy? "It does not exist," was the answer. Where is the purgatory of which I have been told so often? "It does not exist." But my friends were in darkness, and a yearning came that I might go to them and tell them what I knew. I wanted to say, "Do not be mistaken; there is something better, brighter, grander, nobler for human souls than has been taught you. I was told that I could return, and became conscious that I could communicate with those still on earth if I found a certain channel, an avenue, an instrument. How could I find it? "All things are yours," is the promise. Therefore I must find the way and the instrument. This I did, and you have helped me. That is the work which I am doing, and it gives me increased happiness.

I was told that there were greater beauties of the spiritual landscape which I had not yet seen, and which I could not yet understand, because the universe is illimitable. There is something over-poweringly grand in the thought that you are not cramped or shut up in a small space of a few millions of miles. No, this universe is vast, and the field is mine to explore. It became mine by right. I had worked for it, and I had yet to work for it. Take special note of that. I was to work and earn the right to explore God's dominions, and get happiness from every place, state, and condition of my spiritual existence.

Do you like grand architecture: From what source do you think that the old Greeks got their first designs? Phidias and Praxiteles were, no doubt, the greatest of Greek sculptors. There were wonderful architects in those days. When I was upon the earth plane, I made a nine months' tour of Greece, Rome, and Sicily to make a study of the architecture of the ancients. I visited every temple, whether in ruins or in perfect order, and I tell you they are heaps of stones, they are utterly beneath contempt compared with the spiritual architecture of the homes and houses in the spirit world. If you have a spiritual body, there is no reason why you should not have a spiritual house. Get rid of the idea that you are a puff of wind in the life hereafter. Even wind may be solidified, for wind is atmosphere in motion, and it is possible to solidify the atmosphere. Then I came to the inhabitants of that spirit world. I had never previously believed or dreamed that these could exist in such beautiful forms. To most people, beauty of form is a source of joy and comfort. The Greeks and the Romans loved beauty of form, and I know that you do likewise. I saw the most exquisite forms as I progressed, and every day, to use language which you will understand, I met with some that I had previously known upon the earth-plane, and what words can tell the joy of it? To some of them I had done little acts of kindness. And let me impress upon you that of all the pleasure I have received on the spirit side of life, the most came from those to whom I had previously done some act of kindness. If I had my earth life again, I would spend every hour in doing good—I would spend my life in doing acts of kindness.

In our spiritual rest houses we frequently meet, not only with loved ones, but with those whom we reverenced and adored. We make also new acquaintances. We get a knowledge of great and grand souls, and come in contact with them. After a time, I was appointed by an Intelligence to do a certain work. I was to help others to see the light, and I had permission to come back to the earth again. Then my instructor said, "That which will g you the greatest pleasure, do." Then I came back.

I have met with many great and noble characters, who lived upon the earth plane. I am frequently in the companionship of those whom I loved, and I have never yet found cause for offence, and never will. No one has entered into my surroundings who has caused me a moment of sadness. On the earth-plane even your best moments are clouded because some one in your midst was objectionable to you; but each one on the spirit side has gravitated to a certain spiritual level. If he be good, then his spiritual status is good, his affinities will be good, and those who come in immediate contact with him will be good also. There will be no one to offend.

So vast are the realms or dominions of Nature that in the few years I have been on the spirit side of life, I have been able to explore but little. When I have been upon the etheric plane for some billions of years I shall perhaps have seen a little of it. But throughout the countless ages of eternity I shall be evolving, developing, getting knowledge and light and wisdom. I shall become in tune with the Infinite.

What there is beyond I do not yet know. Even on our side of life we are not given more knowledge than we can make use of for the time being. It is all a matter of progression. I have told you that we all have to work. There are no drones. But it is work that is congenial and satisfactory; it is a labour of love. It is appointed by a Higher Intelligence; it is given to you to do; and if you do it, your progress and happiness are assured. Realize that there is no coercion on the spirit side of life, but the spiritual eyes are opened to their responsibility. They see everything at a glance. In the spirit side of life you are not left in any doubt. You have full knowledge that to obey is better than to sacrifice, and to do the will of God is to bring happiness in your progressive existence, throughout eternity. Mothers have had their children taken away by death, and the bereaved ones say, "We have lost our children." You have not lost them. They may have been lost from vision for a while. Perhaps there are some here tonight who laid to rest in cold earth a little form, a sweet child. I do not seek to stir up your feelings, but you remember how the burning tears came to your eyes; you rebelled in your soul when a child was taken away. There was an aching void in your heart and you murmured. That life was only taken and planted in another garden, and when you get on the other side, you will know your child. But not as a babe, for all grow to full spiritual stature, radiant, glorious in immortality, with soul filled with love for you, nevermore to part.

Is it not worth striving for? There is no condemnation to those who are good, those who are living the life, those who are seeking to do that which is right. Let me tell you, that the time is coming when all earth problems, religions, and theology, will pass away. Men are tired of such discussions. They are sick in their soul of being told to trust in another; they cannot fathom the scheme or plan of salvation, but they do know that around about them is a world of misery, of unhappiness, of shortcomings. It is only the true spiritual philosophy which teaches man to rely upon himself and become his own saviour by being true to himself. There is no religion higher than truth. To serve God he must serve man. That pleases the Father and continues eternally. We must become servants of each other."

CHAPTER V

I HAVE thought a little and laboured long to comprehend the economy of Nature. I have found life everywhere, in trees and flowers and growing grains, in rapid brooks, and lazy streams, in the wind sweeping over the hills, and at rest in lonely places, in the majesty and glory of the dawn as the sun climbs the eastern sky, in the glow of evening and in the purple solitude of night. I see life seeking better expression and individual growth in every birth, and rocked in every cradle. I see Nature working out its destiny, reproducing, increasing, and developing; and in such a presence I know that nothing, not even death itself, can diminish or stop the eternal progress of a single life, all a part of one stupendous whole.

We speak of inert matter, but there is no such thing in the Universe. Matter, the expression and language of which we do not understand, we term inert,—an error caused by our lack of knowledge. Nothing dead exists. We have little knowledge of

53

the very small, and know nothing of the world of life forms invisible to the human eye,—how they live, what they do, or how they communicate with one another.

There is a query in science as to whether every living thing is capable of thinking, and I am free to say that, in my judgment, wherever there is life, there must be thinking.   I care not whether science accept or reject the theory; there is the power of intelligent action in every seed that has a living germ.   The acorn has sense enough to send its rootlets into the earth, and its trunk and foliage branch up into the air, and select just such elements as will make the oak tree, and reject such as would be proper only for the beech tree.   And the grass has the same kind of intelligence in choosing proper nourishment for itself; and the power of choice must involve the power of thought.   Science is on the material and rudimental plane yet, and has much to ascertain.

Speaking of the life mass, one in the next life has said:

"The basis of all matter is electricity; the basis of all electricity, for there are many kinds, is ether, —not that ether which is found in the atmosphere, but a subtle ether of which men know little or nothing.   The basis of this subtle ether is spirit; therefore, all that there is of whirling planets, of brilliant constellations, suns, moons, and satellites, all that there is in the physical Universe is ether clothed, in reality but an expression of spirit. It is the physical in and through which spirit functions, and in that way makes itself manifest to the external sense. When we once realize how infinitely great is the universe, how wondrous, how terrible, yet how beautiful in its simplicity, a feeling not exactly of awe, but of benign thankfulness must rise in our hearts at the knowledge that we are part of that stupendous system.

"Until the discovery of lenses and magnifying glasses, man had no idea of the world around him. He could not scan the heavens by night, nor did he know anything of the world in a drop of water or in the ice gem. He knew nothing of atoms, nor of micro-organisms.

"If one is interested in geology—in the various rocks in the strata of the earth—let him take the hardest of these rocks—basalt—and in the basaltic rocks he will find a world of life. If he gets far away in the polar seas at the extremes of the earth, he will there find life also. Thousands of fathoms down in the bed of the ocean there is life. In everything throughout the Universe life is found, and the germs of life are no less in the fire mists!

Think of the specks of protoplasm floating in the water. Look at them—examine them with a microscope. Then realize that at last, a long way off it is true, those specks of protoplasm develop into a Shakespeare or a Dante, Thomas Paine or an Ingersoll. Nature is very wonderful!

"The atmosphere that you are breathing to-night contains organisms. You cannot see them with the naked eye, and even the most powerful lenses would fail to disclose some of them to you. There are microbes floating in the atmosphere, some of which produce disease. Most of them are unimportant. But apart from the germs, there are floating throughout this atmosphere, life forms which man may never be able to discover with any instrument that he may invent in the future. Near to Mount Vesuvius there are a few pools or small lakes, which the internal fires round about make very hot. If to-night I could take one drop from those pools and subject it to a close, rigid scrutiny by means of a more powerful glass than exists, we should find that in one drop of this hot water there is a world. We should find life there evolving and progressing towards perfection. Again, we should find in that drop of water, or it might be in a speck of earth—if we had the knowledge and power, and also the sight of an advanced spirit to disintegrate it—we should find that the speck of matter branches away into electric corpuscles. Searching deeper, we should discover that even the electricity of the corpuscles is made up of a subtle ether, impenetrable, something so rarefied that the sons of men cannot by any means discern it. Had we the power and the knowledge that we shall have some day in an advanced spiritual state, we should find in the heart of that subtle ether something of wondrous power and influence—a continuous force which is indeed the Spirit of God.

"Therefore, in the physical we have a universe which at last touches the spiritual. In the infinitely great we have a universe which is controlled, inspired, kept steady, so to speak, and has its foundation, its very existence, in that force called Nature. And the spirit which you yourselves possess, is an emanation from God. This Spirit, though manifest in many ways, and through many forms, is eternal. Matter physical is constantly changing, building up, disintegrating; it is scattered and reformed in the birth, the growth, the life, and the death of worlds innumerable. There is, in reality, no such thing as death. Men enquire from whence comes life? Life came from the Spirit, and when the spirit passes through the subtle ether, and the ether gets into the coarser electricity, it takes physical form—gross matter is then impregnated with life.   That life never ceases, because, as I have said, it progresses and develops through the physical and is re-absorbed into the Great Spirit, the Source of all life—light, and power, and wisdom."

Another from the great beyond has said:—

"In the whole universe right down to the microscopic and beyond, life is found.   There is no part of the universe where there is no life, nor where creatures do not live in companies.   It is not good for man, or anything to be alone; consequently all are set in companies, and there has been given to each individual a method and a way of understanding every other one, so that all may be happy in one another's company.   Some will say that it is ridiculous to speak of inanimate things in that manner, but it is only ignorance which so asserts; it is inability to realize that the Divine Spirit of God is permeating everything.   Walk upon the sands of the sea-shore, examine the tiniest grain; it is impregnated with that Divine Spirit which keeps the whole universe sweet.

"I cannot say much concerning the manner of communication that plants have, but I know from my side of life that they have this power, and do communicate.   And the varieties of perfumes, how are they produced, and borne upon the breeze? The present hypothesis is that it is through some chemical atoms. First, the sun impregnated the plant. In the flower are found chemical substances—electrons—which are given off and float on the subtle ether. How do they float? Through vibrations. We have been a long time getting a little knowledge about vibrations, but the processes of Nature are carried on through vibrations. We have thought it most wonderful to set in motion electrical vibrations, and convey to our friends a message hundreds of miles away. That is but a childish effort, a childish accomplishment in comparison with what goes on daily around us, but of which we are ignorant. Realize first that there is the life of the plant, and there is the life of the animalcule, the life of the insect, the life of the animal, the life of man, and the life of creatures in the uttermost parts of Nature of which most men have no conception. Then we come to the Sources of all Life,— God. Cannot we understand that from Him flows the entire life of the Universe? When we die, as the expression is, though such a thing does not happen—when a dissolution of the material body and the spirit occurs, what takes place is this: there is a breaking up of a community—you and your body are a community interdependent on each other,—and at death, or dissolution, a colony, a company breaks up—I must for the time-being use terms which will be understood—the etheric tenant vacates and goes on to a more glorious, sublime plane. Paul said to the Corinthians, "There is a natural body, and there is a spiritual body." It is the earthly house of the tabernacle here which dissolves.

The companies of insects, and of animals, though they make war on each other and may exist on each other, have a language. They know how to communicate, and in a measure they are dependent one upon the other. Is it not amusing to hear some people say that man alone has speech, that is, sound formed into certain words and syllables and sentences through the vocal organs? Let us, for instance, consider the birds. We see them and hear them warble and sing. That is their way of expressing joyousness; but that is not their language. They have a way in which they communicate with each other just as we have. Has the reader ever visited India? In the Burning Ghaut, where the Hindoos and others burn their dead, they carry the bodies up a flight of stairs to a high platform. The wood is already prepared, and the body is placed upon the wood. Look up into the heavens, calm and bright, the sun glaring down, not a speck in the sky. In two or three minutes the place will be black with carrion birds. Can we explain it? Yes, away perched on some high eminence or tree is the sentinel bird; perhaps miles away are his fellows. He speaks to them, the sentinel sounds the signal, and instantly they reply to him, and fill the air. Most people think that the world in which they live is a jumble. I grant that there are things that are abhorrent, which we cannot understand—the mystery of pain and suffering, of evil, for example, but I realize now that out of all that is evil, will finally come good. There is no confusion or jumble in the Divine Order. Everything is in its place, and ultimately it will be seen that in Nature, God has set the solitary in families, that His wondrous power is always recreating matter, and that there is never annihilation.

There may, however, be change of form. Take, for instance, the coral rocks on the seashore. Little creatures once swam in the ocean in tiny shells; they died in myriads, and the shells in time formed certain rocks. Old forests fall in decay, and the wisest man of the 20th century might have said: "Show me the wisdom of God in this?" But to-day the coal formed from these forests is used to give warmth and light, and all the processes of commerce are carried on through it.

There is no death!   Everything gives place to new forms of life.

And this is the fact that we must gather from our teaching: that out of the life contained in the mass, individuality has come; out of the mass of life, through Nature's process of constant change and refinement, every living creature that will inhabit this globe in the ages yet to come must be evolved.   The highest form of life that is evolved from the mass is man—and to the highest, all lesser forms contribute.   Mankind is the final result of evolutionary action.

CHAPTER VI

THE CONTINUITY OF LIFE

DO the so-called dead actually live beyond the grave? If so, where? Can they communicate with us after they have left their physical bodies? Have conditions been perfected by which they can talk to those living here, using their own voice? Do their words sound the same in our atmosphere as they did when they inhabited their physical bodies?" These questions and many more have often been asked me. I answer, "Yes"—but the abstract affirmative reply means so little that I propose to give a detailed explanation of the facts. If I can explain the principle involved, the result will be understood, for the former is a condition depending upon the latter.

We were conducting our investigation as usual. The room devoted to the purpose was in intense darkness, as it always was, and the atmospheric movement was slow. Mrs. French, my assistant, the most perfect psychic then living, was with me.

In the darkness appeared points of non-luminous light, constantly in motion, cloudy, etheric substance, half-form, which moved with an effect of a cool wind blowing across one's face and hands, as it passed and repassed.   A strong influence seemed to take some vital force from me.

From years of similar experience I knew that aiding us was a group of workers in the after-life, who were creating conditions by which it would be possible for them, and those whom they would bring, to converse with us; that etheric and physical matter were being transformed into a state in which they could be used to clothe the vocal organs of spirit people.

"Do spirit people have bodies?" is a question frequently asked. My answer is that they have, and when in this world, it is clothed with a flesh garment. In the change the etheric body discards the flesh covering, but that act does not destroy the individual, or his etheric body, or his organs of speech, or change them in any way. The flesh covering of man's etheric body makes possible existence in the physical world. Similarly, the absence of the flesh garment makes possible his existence in the spirit world. It is only by again clothing organs of speech with matter slow in vibration that the words of inhabitants of the etheric world may sound in our atmosphere, and after this has been done, an individual in the after-life has no more difficulty in speaking than he had when in the earth-life. These were the conditions being arranged on the evening which I am about to describe.

As we waited, every faculty was alert. Though I had had the same experience upon hundreds of previous occasions, yet each occasion seemed more interesting and different from the one preceding. I had long since ceased to demand tests, or to insist on the coming of any particular individual. I asked for knowledge, and any one who was in a position to give that would, I knew, talk; so with patient expectation we waited, conversing easily, filling the room with voice vibrations. Who out of the great beyond could take on the physical condition which would make conversation possible?

There was absolute silence, save for a slight movement as of soft garments, a moment of expectancy as we awaited the greeting of those from the great beyond—was there ever a situation more intensely interesting?

"Good evening, Mr. Randall. I am glad to have the pleasure of greeting Mrs. French again." The voice was clear and distinct. "I have been asked to tell you something of the conditions that make speech possible.

"First of all," he continued, "I know that to your physical eyes all is in intense darkness. With us, however, who no longer live subject to physicial vibrations, there is light, but not the light of your day.   To us in the etheric world, who are not bound by earth conditions, all is light—a state far different from the light you know.   In our light the physical is visible, and through it we pass as easily as atoms pass through your solids, and here let me say, as we have often said before, our etheric bodies are just as perfect as when we inhabited physical garments in the earth plane, or as your bodies are to-night.   When compared to yours, our bodies appear transparent, and all things in this life appear more transparent than did things in the earth plane, but they are more real to us than things physical are to you, because more intense. It is difficult, I know, with all you have been told, to comprehend matter, except it be tangible—but to continue my account of the work being done here.

"From Mrs. French's brain project magnetic lines of force, to me perfectly visible, extending to a point just over the table between you, while over your head appears a bar of light from which other lines of force reach out, meeting those first described, under which there appears to be a cup into which the magnetic and electric forces so taken are gathered. These substances, etheric in character, are by chemists, skilled in such work, manipulated to clothe my organs of speech; otherwise the sound of my voice would not fall upon your ears. All psychics possess a peculiar vital force that is used by us; otherwise they would not be psychics, and when I speak to you I am for the moment really an inhabitant of your world, just as for the moment you are in touch with the after-life. In the conditions prevailing at this moment, there is no line of demarcation between the so-called two worlds; we are both in the same room, actually within a few feet of each other; both have bodies; for the moment, you sit in a chair, while I stand, and each hears the other's words. If I could gather just a little more strength, I could touch you."

"Just a moment," I interrupted, "won't you take my hand in order that I may feel the tangibility of an etheric body, re-clothed for the moment?"

"I will try," was the answer. "Wait."

Then in the darkness I held one hand to my right, while across the table at right angles my left held firmly both hands of my assistant. This was in a room in my own residence; all light was excluded, and we were alone. Soon a hand took

mine; there was no groping.   I took the hand meeting my own firmly, feeling the form and outline.
It was warm, and perfectly natural in all respects
with one exception; although it rested easily, yet it
seemed to move and to vibrate beyond any description I can give.   As my hand closed, the other hand
seemed to dissolve.   No word was uttered during
that particular time.   Then the gentleman speaking from a point very near his former position,
said:

"We do not like to use the material that we have
gathered with such great effort for physical demon-
strations, for so much can be accomplished in other
ways.   Do you know there is no place in the world
to-day where such work can be done, as in your
home to-night?   I mean that working with Mrs.
French and you so long, we have overcome many
crude conditions, and have reached such a state of
perfection that many of those in an advanced plane
can enter, can teach laws and explain conditions
unknown among men, touching the very foundation
of the physical.   Then again, working in conjunction with you, we bring many persons into that
quasi-physical, quasi-etheric condition which is
necessary to restore them to a conscious state.
We do a work that is being accomplished in
no other place; here the physical and the etheric

force blend as one, and here many of the dead, so-called, are awakened in the conditions created. We shall always feel the obligations we owe you, for with your aid we have helped very, very many in the years gone by, the extent of which you have little idea."

From this it would seem that physical vibrations, working in conjunction with the etheric are necessary to create a condition where some in the after-life may be roused from an unconscious state. If this be so

"Earth needs Heaven, but Heaven indeed
Of Earth has just as great a need."

"We can help you, and you can help us in so many ways," he said.

"How do our physical bodies appear to you to-night?" I inquired.

"Your bodies, I now speak of the flesh covering," he said, "may be likened to a lighted pumpkin on Hallowe'en night. Some give out more light than others, depending on the development and refinement of the life force. Generally speaking, a physical covering appears dark, some darker than others. The life force in many is fine, in others undeveloped; there is as much difference as in the arc light and the candle,

"Your brain." he continued, "appears to me like a fine machine in constant motion. As suggestions both spirit and physical, through movement of matter reach you, they pass into the brain machine, are fashioned and changed, then flow out in new form, and we of this world not only see them enter but we see them emerge. All in the world is substance and all is life; they are one and the same thing, for life has never existed and never can exist without substance; form cannot be without matter; so in this way we illustrate how important it is to keep the thought, the output of the brain clean, and men and women will keep it clean when they come to know that it is visible. But I am transgressing; there are others who would speak—good night."

"I have waited," the voice of a woman then said, "so long for just the conditions to prevail that would enable me to speak. To-night, while the gentleman was addressing you, I was told by those having the work in charge that I might try. I was asked to stand to the right of the table that separates the psychic from you. This I did when the chemist of the spirit group took from the cup in which it had been gathered, a substance slow in vibration and precipitated the material around and about my organs of speech. I touched my mouth and moved my tongue, both seemed in a way different, but their use was not modified, and when I spoke to you I realized that my voice sounded the same as it did before I left your world.

"My passing out of the old body was so delightful, so different from what I had expected, and the plane in which I now live is so wonderful that I have long been anxious to give to your world a description of my going and of what awaited me. I now see that I lived a fairly good life. As occasion presented, I did what little I could to make those about me happier, helped those less fortunate as opportunity offered, and tried to do right. I had no knowledge of what followed the earth-life, but I always had an abiding faith that if people invariably did the best they could, all would be well, and I was not disappointed.

"In my last illness, as the hour of dissolution approached, I felt no fear. It seemed to me that I was about to make a natural change, and that in some place I should live on in the companionship of those who had preceded me. There came over me a weakness that I cannot describe; I seemed to sleep. With great effort I aroused my faculties, and plainly saw members of my household, some kneeling about the bed sobbing. I wanted to speak to them, but found I was unable to articulate. Looking again I was for a moment startled, for I saw many faces of spirit people smiling. Looking once more, I saw beside my bed my dear husband, whose face was full of tenderness, and who took my hand speaking words of welcome. Others whom I now know help on such occasions, gathered about me, their hands under my poor physical body, encouraging me, and telling me all was well. Soon, without any effort on my part, for I was far too weak to make an effort, I seemed to be lifted above and out of my old body, and stood among the others referred to, startled at the reality.

"I turned and saw the old flesh body, white and still, and heard the cry of anguish as the physician said, 'She is dead.'   I wanted to speak to the loved ones who mourned, and tell them, as I do now that I was not dead, but conscious and living.   I was informed, however, that my words would fall upon deaf ears, and that in my present disturbed mental state the wisest course would be for me to go with my husband to a rest house for a little time, until I should grow accustomed to the change.   Later, I was told, I should be shown the beauty of the afterlife, and in good season should come again into the house of mourning.   I was not for one moment unconscious in passing from one world to the other.

"Many of those who had preceded me into the

after-life, who came to help in the change, went with us to the house of rest; there was great joy among them, but my heart was filled with sorrow, for many dear ones left in your world needed a mother's care. I could not at that time comprehend the wisdom of the infinite, or realize that each change in Nature means progress. I will not undertake," she continued, "to describe the joy of meeting with those who had preceded me, or of the coming and going of friends and acquaintances. Their good cheer and happiness were a great comfort, but my thoughts were ever with those in the old life who grieved so much. I felt that I must go and tell them, but I was informed that the time was not opportune, for they were without knowledge. Further, I was assured that both they and I must learn many things before help would be possible, except by suggestion, and that I should be instructed in good time.

"What impressed me most after a period of rest, and my faculties had become alert, was the reality of all things. I looked at my own body, which seemed as tangible as before the change, although it had perhaps a more etheric appearance. I stood upon my feet, and moved my legs, arms, and head; my senses of touch, smell, and sight were more acute; I spoke to those about me, and they answered; I looked over a valley and saw running brooks, and lakes, trees, grass, and flowers of many kinds.   I took long deep breaths of wonderfully vitalizing air, and as the new conditions dawned upon me, I turned to those about me questioningly.

" 'I do not understand,' I said.

" 'No,' they answered, 'as you have never been taught anything concerning this life, how could you understand?   But let us tell you one fact: the life you have now entered is just as material as the one you have left.   Stop for a moment and realize that truth.   Moreover, everything in the earth-plane is only a poor imitation of a part of what exists in this plane.'

" 'Did it never strike you as absurd,' a spirit said, 'that houses, trees, flowers, and all animal life should be limited to the physical plane; such a proposition must assume that the universe is limited to the earth planet?'

" 'I could not grasp the suggestion,' I said, and I asked that I might rest for a while.   Turning my head, I saw the smiling face of my husband beckoning, and I went with him with confidence, as in the days of youth.

"I am weary now," she said, "the material seems to be falling from my lips and throat; there is so much that I want to say; I will come again."

Her strength was exhausted, with the experience half told.

"You have said that in the world of spirit, you have lands and waters, lakes and rivers, trees and shrubs, vines and flowers; tell us of them in language we may comprehend," I said to another spirit who greeted us.

"In the first place," he answered, "you must disabuse your mind of the idea that nothing existed before your poor earth-planet came into being, or that nothing exists beyond the physical. The truth is that all things which in the ages have found expression on the earth-plane, have existed in the etheric world since the beginning. There were rivers flowing down from mountains, and lakes in the valleys among the hills, and lands and trees and embracing vines, and flowers long before this planet was fertile, and now only a few of the wonderful things of our plane are able to find expression in yours. Then again, there is much vegetation developing in our etheric material that the earth in its crude state cannot clothe, and your inability to comprehend vegetation beyond or outside the earth lies in the fact that you have heretofore had an erroneous idea that all life originated in the physical."

CHAPTER VII

A UNIVERSE OF MATTER

A JUST and full appreciation of the fact that the Universe is composed of Matter in varying degrees of activity is a condition precedent to a true comprehension of the great problem of life. Through it we can understand dissolution and learn something of the conditions prevailing beyond the physical.

The suggestion that the whole Universe is Material, and the different spheres are, in fact, substance with varying vibration and intensity, and that individual life continues in those different planes similar to life in our plane, is startling, but no more so than the advancement of the Copernican theory, or the discovery of the law of gravitation. It took hundreds of years for the acceptance of the first proposition, and upon the enunciation of the second the jealous ones said that the grand laws of universal gravitation deduced by Newton were false. Much time will necessarily elapse before the following propositions are accepted, that the whole Universe is material, and that all space is filled and peopled. The reason for this delay is that man's mental process is slow, and a new discovery is only accepted finally after repeated demonstration.

It is an axiom in physics that matter only acts on matter, so if mind acts on matter, mind itself must be matter. One experiences great difficulty in approaching a fact so new—there is difficulty in finding words with which to express the proposition in simple language. Words are as limited as knowledge on the subject; so when we go beyond the beaten path, we must give new meaning to old words or invent new ones. Matter, as that term has been heretofore understood, is confined substantially to things tangible and physical. This is too limited a use, for if the universe is material, matter does not cease to be when it ceases to be tangible.

I would put the facts in this way:

(a) Matter slow in action is subject to the law of gravitation, and therefore physical.

(b) Matter so rapid in vibration as not to be subject to the law of gravitation is etheric.

Matter when it ceases to be physical is only changed in density. Certain forms of matter may be changed by chemical action and advanced to the spiritual state; then by the reduction of atomic motion the same matter may be restored again to its former condition, to hold once more physical expression. Mind is matter raised to its highest degree of atomic activity when it holds within itself inherent power of intelligent direction. Every atom, every electron and molecule has form, and when those atoms, electrons, and molecules, by attraction, are so closely drawn together as to become tangible, they still have individual form. When by Nature's process they are advanced step by step until they become etheric, they still have form; the mind which is etheric has form, is substance; it is real, and its creations take definite shape. Mind acts on matter, as we use the homely phrase; that is to say, matter raised to its highest degree of activity utilizes the tangible substances necessary to give physical expression. This is demonstrated in each individual, for the mind directs the body, and the physical body obeys the will of the spirit.

When the statement is made that life continues beyond the grave, the average thinking man doubts it. When the suggestion is put forth that we have now and here a spirit body, which in dissolution only separates from the physical, the assertion is not understood. When the statement is put forth

that there is continuity of this life, and that spirit
people have bodies, live in a material universe, and
have homes similar to our own, the words mean
nothing to the average person, for such conditions
are beyond comprehension.

In order that these propositions may be understood, it is necessary to explain the conditions
which make such a state possible; we must know
the law through which life holds continuity.
Therefore, a just and true comprehension of the
following facts is essential, there is a material universe beyond the physical; there is an etheric universe within and outside the physical; and the entire universe is composed of matter in different
states of vibration or modes of motion. These
truths must be understood before a single individual can comprehend the continuity of life—
that the so-called dead have bodies, form, feature,
and expression, and that they live on intelligently
in a world as material as this, continuing their
progression. Everything that possesses the property of *gravitation* or *attraction* is classed as matter. That is the most scientific definition of matter given by people in the world beyond this.
Matter is either solid, liquid, or gaseous. If solid,
it is strongly cohesive. If liquid, less so. If
gaseous, the atoms may be said to bump against

each other and rebound. Molecules are made up of several atoms. For instance, a molecule of water is composed of three atoms, two of hydrogen and one of oxygen. Atoms are smaller particles of matter, possessed of forces so wonderful that it is utterly impossible to trace them down and examine them, for the reason that they are continually changing, so rapid is their passage through the atmosphere.

There is much the scientists do not know about atoms. About two hundred miles above this earth plane extends what we call atmosphere at which distance it becomes very rare. What then extends throughout the universe, throughout the solar system—throughout all solar systems? There exists something which is not like the earth's atmosphere, which is called Ether, through which, with vibrating undulating motion, come waves of light, ultimately reaching the earth plane, giving not only light but life. These countless atoms are in constant motion, passing through the Ether, with wave-like undulatory motion, having perfect form, with individual likes and dislikes. They have intelligence, are drawn together, or there is no affinity, for through affinity there is cohesion. Cohesion among the atoms, when slow, becomes physical and visible. That cohesion may be among etheric atoms, where the vibration of the mass is so rapid that it has to us no visibility. The cohesion of atoms is not confined to the physical world, for, through the universal law, these atoms find expression not only in but beyond the physical. The two planes of consciousness are closely inter-woven. The same law that governs and controls and directs the one, governs and controls and directs the other. It is only, therefore, through the law that we are able to advance out of the physical.

Every atom has force, and force wherever found or however expressed is life, and every atom has heat—heat so intense that all the furnaces of this earth could not reproduce it. This Ether, this subtile substance permeates all things physical.

One of the great impediments to our realization of spirit presence and activity is our inability to conceive force and matter in their more refined forms not manifest to the physical senses or sus-ceptible to touch or vision. Yet all the greatest forces are unseen. Electricity, magnetism, and steam are only cognizable to our vision by their occasional manifestation of light and colour, or through the vapour produced by the latter when it meets with the atmosphere.

Changing the vibratory condition or density of water by heat illustrates in a simple way the proposition herein stated. You take a basin of water and put a fire under it; it commences to bubble, its motion increases, its vibration is raised; it changes to steam. By confining that steam, and applying more heat, super-heated steam, which in itself is invisible, results. This passes from our vision, but is not lost or destroyed, for by another process we can restore it to its original state. Again, the sun causes evaporation of the waters; they pass and become etheric and a part of the world—invisible, but through Nature's process of condensation they fall again as rain. By that process the water did not cease to be, but by that change it ceased to be visible. While invisible, its density was changed, its vibration slowed, and it became once more subject to the laws of gravitation.

Again, every atom that forms the mass has not only form, but energy, and force, which is life. Life may be so low as to be beyond our appreciation, or its development may be so high as to be equally beyond our comprehension. In the cohesion of the atoms through their affinity and their development, we find the varied expressions of life. Evolution is a constant force, an inherent desire for development, and that great law influences every form of life. It is not confined to the physical, but acts upon the grosser substances, and through it they develop and increase.

The Universe did not commence with the birth of this planet; its birth was not the commencement of creation. Our dissolution will not end our individuality. There is around and about us a great universal force that we characterize as Good. That force is a reality, a substance composed of matter, developed beyond the physical, and in every instance where an atom of that force is clothed with grosser material, Nature increases its sum total. We do not have to go beyond the physical universe to see spirit activity. We never see anything else.

At the instant of man's conception, an etheric atom becomes clothed. It takes on through Nature's process, a flesh garment. The sensitive spirit body, like the seed sown in the soil, commences its development in the dark, where it grows and increases in form and stature. The flesh garment is correspondingly increased, and at such times as it becomes able to withstand the light there is a natural birth. The process of growth that commenced at the moment of conception is continuous, it attracts other atoms slow in vibration, it organizes the physical body so that the flesh garment may increase for its uses and purposes. Further, the outer garment wastes from hour to hour, day to day, and week to week, completely changing once in every few years. But the individual having form, feature, and expression does not change except to increase mentally and physically.

If the whole Universe is composed of matter, man both spiritual and physical, is not an exception to the universal law. The physical eye cannot see the etheric spirit in the body, nor can it see the spirit out of the body. If the spirit in the earth life is not composed of matter, how would it be possible to hold form, feature, and expression? This is the keynote to understanding, for with a comprehension of that proposition we can appreciate what dissolution is, and we may finally understand that every plane in which we live is a reality, and composed of matter.

Within certain vibratory action, matter is physical, tangible, and visible, and subject to the law of gravitation. When vibration is increased beyond that point, we are in the domain of spirit where one is not subject to the laws of gravitation. The line of demarcation, therefore, between the spiritual and the physical is that point where the law of gravitation ceases to have influence. The whole spirit world, as well as the life force that functions in the tangible in this world is made up of etheric matter, as distinguished from physical matter. When the gross matter is refined to a certain point, it becomes and ever remains Ether, but all is matter technically in different modes of motion, or in different states of vibration.

This proposition is so new in physics, so beyond the experience of men, that it is difficult to grasp, but it can and will be understood through the research of the physicist who without fear of the criticisms of our world calls to his aid those few psychics who have developed the sixth and seventh senses, and are able to see and hear what is said and done in the world beyond this—or who, as I have done, have created a condition where the inhabitants of the place beyond can speak to us voice to voice.

CHAPTER VIII

AGAIN a night of experimental work. As I closed the shutters, the stars shone with unusual brilliancy. The atmospheric conditions were perfect—clear, cold, dry, and still. As I shut out the light, seating myself opposite Mrs. French, clouds within the room for a moment seemed to form and roll like smoke from a great fire. Soon they passed away, and non-luminous points of light became apparent and slowly floated. Then there appeared above my head the ribbon or bar of magnetic substance that is always present when the conditions are right for speech with those beyond. Mrs. French through her psychic sight saw a great number of people passing and repassing, while chemists manipulated the etheric and physical material into the exact condition for use in speech.

While waiting for the work to begin, I recall trying to fix the line of demarcation between the two worlds. In a moment I should hear the voices of those actually living in another plane, and they would hear mine. I should speak to them and they to me. They would see me perfectly, though I could not see them. Sight is about the only quality possessed by spirit people in the conditions prevailing which is denied me. After a moment's reflection I realized the limitation of our sight at all times. Such situations make one think deeply.

"Good evening, Mr. Randall." A deep masculine voice broke the stillness. It was not the voice of Mrs. French, nor were her vocal organs of speech used by another. She being deaf, often failed to hear the voices of spirit people and spoke while others were speaking, such interruption sometimes causing confusion. "We have," the voice of one of the directors of our group continued, "a great work to do to-night, and as atmospheric conditions are unusual, we have gathered a great throng in substantially the same mental attitude, and have brought them here for help. You have done this work so long that you, of course, understand that these people do not as yet know that they have separated from their old physical bodies and are no longer inhabitants of Earth. Won't you talk to them? They are living so much in your plane as yet that you can secure and hold their attention more closely than we can."

This was not a new experience. My records show upwards of 700 nights when this particular character of work had been done. As requested, I commenced to talk easily and naturally. I could not see, but Mrs. French could always see spirit people gather about listening, and some would come close watching me intently, while others would discuss among themselves softly so as not to interrupt my talk; they were evidently trying to comprehend the situation. I had long ago learned that those whom we were endeavouring to help must not be startled or frightened, as such shock would break the conditions that enabled them to speak; and therefore on this night I discussed generally the unusual situations presented at this particular meeting, leading slowly up to the great change that had taken place. Had I bluntly told those assembled that they were all dead, the shock would probably have ended the work for the night. I have often known this to occur.

It had been my observation that some man among those assembled could take on material that would enable him to talk, and in that manner rivet the attention of all those who listened, and this night was no exception to the rule.

"I have," a strong voice remarked, "been deeply impressed with what you have said, but I do not comprehend its import. Death is a subject that I did not like to think about; people generally give the subject little if any attention, and of course enter the next life ignorantly. I am afraid I am no exception to the rule. If I am to infer that such a change has come into my life, I am wholly unprepared."

"Tell me," I answered, "what you now observe, for I assume your vision is clear."

"For sometime I have been watching the preparations being made. Substance appearing like bars of light about you and the lady opposite was being worked and woven into place. Then I looked about and saw a great company gathered. One of those who seemed directing affairs asked me to permit material to be precipitated upon me so that I might talk to you. This was done without my understanding the process or import. Tell me the meaning of this procedure, if you please."

"I am deeply interested," I said, "in the progress of man, after death so-called, and with the aid of this lady and the group you saw working with us I am able, when conditions are favourable, to have speech with those beyond the earth-plane."

"I gathered that from your first talk," he answered, "but all is so natural with me that it is hard to believe we are not in the old body, for we are like yet unlike. Those who seem to control the situation have bodies from which radiates light, while my own and those of all who are gathered listening, seem enveloped in something like a mantle of darkness; not that exactly, for we are surrounded by what I should describe as a dark, intangible substance carried by the individual as he moves. If, as you say, all these whom I see except this lady and yourself are living in the world of spirit, why do we differ so much?"

"The appearance," I replied, "is the result of a process of refinement. I don't mean in manner or speech, but in soul or spirit development. In the life you now live, the law of attraction holds full dominion, and all those who enter are irresistibly drawn into that mental state or condition that will accord with their own. That is what I am told. You will find, the intellectual, the high minded, the spiritual, the selfish, the wicked and the immoral, all of them in different groups and in conditions as varying as character. There is no progress from one to another except by a purifying process through labour and suffering until the individual is qualified for advancement. This is a very natural and a very just process, is it not?"

"The suggestion is very new," he remarked. "I cannot say that it is not just, but I do say it is novel.

I never thought of things in that way. If what you say is true, why has it never been taught before?"

"I could answer your question in many ways," I said. "Knowledge is the one thing in the world we have to work for. You can't steal, buy, inherit, or beg it; it must be acquired by effort. Now, as the world generally speaking has never made any genuine effort to obtain knowledge of the conditions prevailing beyond, it is not surprising that men and women don't know. Again," I added, "the average mentality would not, could not, and will not understand, even if I should relate what is being done and accomplished this mmute; but there are some thinkers, and their number is fast increasing, who can and will accept a plain statement of fact when it appeals to their reason."

"I am thinking," he said, "as I never did before, and I don't believe I could have comprehended that the death-change could be so natural, and so simple. What is beyond I don't, of course, know. I seem to be just waking, I realize that I am a living entity in no way changed. I now see I am no longer like you. While you have been talking, those whom I knew in earth-life have come and told me I have made a great change. That is about all I know now."

At this moment another spirit speaking said; "You, my friend, have much to learn. Come with me for a little time for reflection; I want you to appreciate that with all your wealth you were a selfish man. The world was not enriched by your journey through it, and this accounts for the gloom that envelops you and all those who come with you. The first task that you must learn to do is to live for and help others, a process which humanizes and broadens the soul, and develops the man."

Again the silence as the voice ceased. I had an easy discussion with Mrs. French for a time. Then there was a whisper; involuntarily I leaned forward, listening intently that no word from out of the unknown land should be lost, and with a slow and measured voice scarcely above a whisper, a woman said:—

"I cannot understand the wisdom of creation. It seems with my limited experience so unnecessary that there should be so much sorrow and suffering in my world as well as in yours. I am told by teachers greatly advanced that humanity, in working out its destiny, having become selfish, has lost sight of the great object of earth-life. Dominated too much by greed, mankind has wandered away from the path of purpose. You come in contact with so much unhappiness in your work,—for only the unfortunate need the help that you, working with the wonderful groups, can give, that I am permitted to come and speak to you, and to others through you, of the beauty of this land in which we live, to enable you and others to avoid erroneous impressions of all conditions prevailing among us. I came here as an infant before memory recorded events. Like all who live among us I came up from the mass of life and obtained my individuality through conception and birth. My first recollection is of a home similar to yours, except more beautiful; I was mothered by those denied motherhood while living among you. It was all very sweet and tender, without discord or inharmony of any character, but I was taken while yet a baby to the earth-mother, and in her arms while she slept, I absorbed the real mother love. If mothers could only know how children though gone cling to them, how happy they would be, and how glad we are when an earth-mother feels our presence and responds in word or thought! As I grew to girlhood, I was given teachers who helped my mental growth, similar to what I see in your life, except that we are not taught by rule. The capabilities of each are ascertained, and each is helped and directed along the lines of his adaptability, and so life as it is unfolded grows more wonderful and beautiful each day. But I must visit you from time to time and by coming in touch with physical conditions obtain that experience which was lost in leaving your world so young.

"Let me impress upon you the charm of our land by saying that I have never yet found a single one who had emerged and come up out of the earth conditions who wanted to go back, inhabit a flesh garment again, and live among you,—and this regardless of earth ties."

"Tell me more of the actualities of your daily life," I asked.

"You think," she answered, "that you have vision, but your eyes have never looked upon life itself. You think you have hearing, but your dull ears have never heard one strain of our divine music. You have taste, but your tongues have never touched the essence. You have smell, and the aroma of roses carried by etheric atoms fills the nostrils, but you cannot appreciate the perfumes of this land of ours. You feel the touch of the coarse covering of living form without having any conception of the delight of touching life itself. In this sphere we have opportunities for education, joys, and happiness unthought of by you in the earth-land, but these are only for those who have come out of the gross material condition in which they were born. We live in homes largely in groups where harmony of thought and action is perfect, but we too have as many grades of people as do you, and in our earth-condition is found degradation as great as that which you know. Here are found the ignorant, the wicked, the immoral, and the vile. Dissolution does not improve or uplift character; that must come from the germ of good in the heart of every living creature.

"Tell those who fear the end," the voice said, "that what they call death is very wonderful and beautiful; that with us, as with you, though you know it not, love is the one great force in the universe; it is the motor that drives the world and causes action. All things are done in and through it, and because of it. Affinity so-called is the process through which the love-force finds expression. But in this connection let me suggest that love is good, and of God, and walks in the path of honour, never into dishonour. It never brought unhappiness; it is never 'born of lust?'

"It has been a joy and a privilege to speak to you to-night, for if any words of mine can help or make happier a single soul, that joy is reflected about me, and I am happier for having made others happy. Such is the law of God, and the secret of the world. Good night."

What am I to do with such teachings?   Shall I, coward-like, fearing the censure of this little world, hide from men what has been given me? Such actual experiences have convinced me that this individual life continues on and on, through the ages.   If this be so, no tongue should be tied, voice hushed, or hand fail to write of facts so important to the peace and happiness of the human race.

CHAPTER IX

ATOMIC LIFE

IN the mentalogical research for the discovery of the life principle, investigators are going far. Surpassing wonderful is the Carl Zeiss ultra-microscope, which uses only the radiating energy within the portion of the solar spectrum which is beyond the violet. These waves are so rapid they do not affect the retina and are hence invisible, but they do activate silver emulsions on highly sensitive plates. Inconceivable minute life, living atoms, or bodies in motion are photographed on rapidly moving films. The result is beyond imagination. When these long strips of successive radiographs are illuminated by strong electric light, under a powerful projecting lens, uncounted thousands of unknown kinds of living atoms are seen moving with intense activity.

De Vries designates these minute particles concealed in living matter, "pangens," and says that "they are quite another order than chemical molecules; that each must grow and multiply by self-division " These pangens are probably units containing mind, and if so, his opinion gives a mind cast to the Universe and all that it includes.

I cite these two scientists to show the tendency of the modern investigator, and to illustrate how far beyond the comprehension of man is the life pangen. Those learned investigators living and working beyond the physical plane, having had greater opportunity to carry on research, go far beyond earthly experiences, because they have had a greater opportunity to acquire knowledge of the fundamental principles of Nature, and it is from this source that I have gathered the information that forms the basis of this work.

It is very difficult at the coming of dawn to say just when the night ends and the day begins. It is impossible to say where one color ends and another begins in the rainbow. It is likewise very difficult to draw the line of demarcation between the physical or tangible, and the etheric or the spiritual. The one is tangible and the other intangible; the one is measured by three dimensions and comprehended by the five senses; the other is demonstrated by clairvoyancy and clairaudiency, the sixth and seventh senses.

I deal now with the part the physical atom plays in the economy of Nature, leaving the etheric, no less material but higher in its vibratory action and functions, to the discussion of etheric form.

We now know that what appears to be solid matter, tangible and dense, which we can see and feel is but an aggregation of physical atoms and molecules slow in vibration, and that within and back of all material is a directive force. One cannot conceive a directive force that does not possess intelligence. Within every atom going to make up the tangible mass is that something called inherent energy or force, which science readily admits, because it is possible to feel and to see the expression of that force. We now go one step further and say that force or energy wherever found, or however expressed, is life, so that we cannot, if we would disassociate energy from life, or force from life, or life from force or energy, simply because they are one and the same thing.

Nature abhors stagnation. Life cannot for one moment be absolutely still; its vibration is so high that there is no inactive substance in the world. That is, every substance has more or less movement, which causes continual change of form and expression. The great law that we call Evolution, influences every atom in the physical world. It is the parent of progress; it is that something inherent in everything from which springs the desire to increase, reproduce, and reach a higher state of development, and that influence is as strong in the atoms and molecules making up what we erroneously call the inanimate mass, as in the animate mass or the individual. We have no conception of the maximum or minimum of motion or movement. The higher the development of the mass, the more rapid its vibration. The lower the mass development, the lower its vibration, the more dark the substance as shown by the spectrum.

It is most difficult to treat a subject so beyond our experience. It is very difficult to explain a condition so far beyond our comprehension, but if we had never interested ourselves in these great unknown forces of Nature, we should not have made the wonderful progress already attained.

It is easy to demonstrate that there is this something called force in all substance going to make up the tangible mass. We take coal, liberate the energy and force therein contained, and utilize it in our industries. We go down into the earth and liberate the gas, bring it to the surface, let it come in contact with fire, that is a substance higher in vibration than the gas itself, and through chemical action we have what we know as combustion; we have released the life-force or the energy; we have dissociated the life-force from the tangible garment. We take water, with heat increase its vibration and convert it into steam, and we have released the energy or life-force contained in the water from its physical garment. And so we could take, were we possessed of greater knowledge, any substance found in the earth, and if we knew how to break down its tangible covering, we would have what science terms "energy," but what I term "life." The life-force, clothed with tangible substance in the process of the alteration that is continually taking place through its affinity for other life-atoms, is constantly changing form, through likes and dislikes, increasing vibratory action to the end that the life-force in the mass may through such continual development and progress reach the highest perfection possible in the physical world, i.e., ultimate physical expression in mankind. In other words, by natural laws, these individual atoms through a process of refinement, through association and dissociation, through likes and dislikes, through chemical combinations and growth, ultimately find expression in the individual.

It has been said that everything in the physical world pays tribute to mankind. It might better be said that everything in Nature, obeying the great universal law of Evolution, when it reaches its highest physical development, finds expression in man.

Every living creature on the face of this globe, was originally an atom, or aggregation of atoms. When it was first clothed, it was so small that no physical eye could discern it, and no magnifying glass could discover it. Its inception was in the dark where the rapid light vibrations could not impede its development. Through the process of growth it was evolved. Vegetables, plants, grains, animals, fish, and many of the birds of the air, through digestive action were utilized to clothe and furnish the physical garment which the individual required in its growth and development. That physical garment is entirely constructed from those tangible substances furnished by the mass, which is necessary for that special purpose, so that we say that the physical form is being constructed out of the mass of matter.

Let us go a step lower, and we find that the physical garment that clothes the vegetable kingdom is taken from the earth-substance still lower. All animal life is constantly taking from the mass the substance which will aid its physical growth. It is all one splendid process of change and growth and progression, all tending toward the apex where stands man the most perfect physical being that Nature seeks to produce in this world.

Looking in the mirror we see reflected not the

individual, but the outer garment of the individual constructed of animal and vegetable matter. In dissolution we simply give back to the fields and to the common earth that which we have temporarily borrowed. The gross material composing our bodies has served its purpose, and it goes back to mother-earth, back into the retort to continue its progression until at some time the substance which covered our etheric form shall reach individuality and then continuity.

Through the labyrinth of creation there is no rest. Vibration is the pulse of Nature. Superficial observation teaches that matter never moves unless acted upon. The sailing ship is propelled by the winds, the engine by steam; there are in Nature endless manifestations of force in moving planets and constellations, in growing vegetation, and in man himself. Motion belongs to the atom. The Universe is but an aggregation of atoms, and its motions are just what those of a single atom placed in its orbit would be. Each atom must be its own motor, and the combined influence of all is the influence of the earth. Mathematical demonstration and deductive reasoning justify this supposition. The agency of an Almighty constantly propelling them, does not meet the demands of reason. Life is born of motion. It is first traceable in the mutual attraction between atoms in solution arranging themselves in definite forms; in affinity and the repulsion of particles. It may appear startling that the forces which create the crystal are living forces; but the data available by known and accepted laws justify the statement.

I would direct attention to the energy contained in the atom. I would impress on the public mind that energy is life, and that all life is material; that is, it is made up of that substance we know as Ether, which is so high in vibration, and so refined that it is not evidential unless clothed with heavier substance which we term physical; moreover, from the life contained in the atom, by evolutionary law, man has evolved. We cannot understand life as expressed in the individual, without knowing at least something of its origin, and the law through which it finds expression in man.

CHAPTER X

DESIRING a clear comprehension of the etheric spheres outside the physical, and having opportunity to speak with one very learned and advanced in the after-life, I said:

"Describe, if you please, the spheres in which you live, with special reference to their tangibility and materiality."

The gentleman answered:

"There are seven concentric rings called spheres. The region nearest the earth is known as the first or rudimental sphere. It really blends with your earth's sphere. It is just one step higher in vibration. Growing more intense and increasing in action are six more, distinguished as the spiritual spheres. These are all concentric zones or circles of exceedingly fine matter encompassing the earth like belts or girdles, each separated from the other and regulated by fixed laws. They are not shapeless chimeras or mental projections, but absolute entities, just as tangible as the planets of the solar system or the earth upon which you reside. They have latitude and longitude, and an atmosphere of peculiarly vitalized air. The undulating currents, soft and balmy, are invigorating and pleasurable."

"How does the landscape appear to you?" I asked.

He answered: "The surface of the zone is diversified. There is a great variety of landscape, some of it most picturesque. We, like you, have lofty mountain ranges, valleys, rivers, lakes, forests, and the internal correspondence of all the vegetable life that exists upon your earth. Trees and shrubbery covered with most beautiful foliage, and flowers of every color and character known to you, and many that you know not give forth their perfume. The physical economy of each zone differs from every other. New and striking scenes of grandeur are presented to us, increasing in beauty and sublimity as we progress."

"Do the seven concentric rings, or spheres, move with the earth as the earth moves?" I asked.

"Although the spheres revolve," he said, "with the earth on a common axis, forming the same angle with the plane of the ecliptic, and move with it about your sun, they are not dependent upon that sun for either light or heat; they receive not a perceptible ray from that ponderable source."

"From what source do you receive your light?" I then asked.

"We receive our light emanations," he said, "wholly from an etheric sun, concentric with your sun, from which central luminary there comes uninterrupted splendour, baffling description. We have, therefore, no division of time into days, weeks, months, or years, nor alterations of season caused by the earth's annual revolution, for the reason that we have no changing season as you have, caused by the action of the sun of your solar system. We, like you, are constantly progressing from day to day, but our ideas of time and seasons differ widely from yours. With you, it is time. With us, it is eternity. In your sphere your thoughts, necessarily bounded by time and space, are limited, but with us thoughts are extended in proportion as we get rid of those restrictions, and our perception of truth becomes more accurate."

"How do you use matter, change its form and condition?" I asked.

"Matter," he said, "with us is only tangible as the mind concentrates upon the object. Then the force of the mind or thought sends its vibration around the object, holding it in a measure tangible. Of course, this is something very different from what you call tangibility. Without this mental concentration the vibration pulses indifferently. That is the natural condition of matter in our zone. It requires the thought to change its form and condition. The vibrating action of matter is measured by the space necessary for the volume."

"How can this material condition in which you live be demonstrated?" I asked.

"One cannot prove," he said, "to a child that steam, that pretty fascinating substance, is harmful until the finger is burned; neither can one instill the truth into an older mind until it is not only opened but has the capacity to comprehend. That all is material in different states of vibration is easily grasped by the thinker. It is impossible to prove by your laws, to actually demonstrate the existence of matter in the higher vibrations in which we live so that men may comprehend. When you deal with matter in the physical, you apply physical laws. When you deal in matter spiritual, you apply spiritual laws, practically unknown among men. The best possible evidence is the vision of the clairvoyant together with deductive reasoning, which, as we have said, is really the highest order of proof.

"Have you ever thought," he said, "that the result of every physical demonstration reaches the consciousness through the avenue of reason? The mentality in a higher state of development comprehends a fact in Nature without physical proof."

"Tell us something of your social life, your scientific research, and religious teaching in the plane in which you reside," I asked.

"With regard to the social constitution of the 'spheres' each is divided into six circles, or societies, in which kindred and cogenial spirits are united and subsist together under the law of affinity. Although the members of each society unite as near as may be on the same plane, agreeing in the most prominent moral and intellectual features; yet it will be found on careful analysis, that the varieties of character in each society are almost infinite, being as numerous as the persons who compose the circle. Each society has teachers from those above, and not infrequently from the higher spheres, whose province is to impart to us the knowledge acquired from their experience in the different departments of science; this, we in turn transmit to those below. Thus by receiving and giving knowledge, our moral and intellectual faculties are expanded to higher conceptions and more exalted views of Nature, the power of which is no less displayed in the constitution of spirit worlds than in the countless resplendent orbs of space. Our scientific researches and investigations are extended to all that pertains to the phenomena of universal truth; to all the wonders of the heavens and of the earth, and to whatever the mind of man is capable of conceiving. All of these researches exercise our faculties and form a considerable part of our enjoyments. The noble and sublime sciences of astronomy, chemistry, and mathematics engage a considerable portion of our attention, and afford us an inexhaustible subject for study and reflection.

"Nevertheless, there are millions of spirits who are not yet sufficiently advanced to take any interest in such pursuits. The mind being untrammelled by the gross material body, and having its mental and intellectual energies and perceptions improved, can by intuition, as it were, more correctly and rapidly perceive and understand the principles and truths on which the sciences are based. In addition to our studies, we have many other sources of intellectual, moral, and heartfelt enjoyment, from which we derive the most ineffable pleasures, some of which are social reunions among children and parents where the liveliest emotion and tenderest affections of our nature are excited, and the fondest and most endearing reminiscences are awakened; where spirit meets in union with spirit, and heart beats responsive to heart.

"We have no sectarian or ecclesiastical feuds, no metaphysical dogmas; our religious teachers belong to that class of persons who were noted during their probation on earth for their philanthropy and deeds of moral bravery; who, regardless of the scoffs and sneers of the time-serving multitude, dared to promulgate and defend the doctrines of civil and religious liberty. They urge upon us, too, the necessity of co-operation in the reformation and advancement of our more degraded brethren by instructing them in the divine principles of love, wisdom, and benevolence. They instruct them in the soul-inspiring and elevating doctrines of universal and eternal progression, and in the sublime truth that evil is not an indestructible and positive principle, but a negative condition, a mere temporary circumstance of existence; and furthermore, that suffering for sin is not a revengeful and malevolent infliction of God, but a necessary and invariable sequence of violated law.

"They teach also that, according to the divine moral economy, there is no such thing as pardon for sins committed—no immediate mercy—no possible escape from the natural results of crime, no matter where or by whom committed; no healing of a diseased moral constitution by any outward appliances, or ceremonial absurdities; and finally, that the only way to escape sin and its consequences, is by progressing above and beyond it."

"What is spirit, as that term is used?" I asked.

"Spirit," he said, "is the one great power in the Universe. The combination of spirit forces is the great power for good, and through the absence of that force many undesirable conditions develop in your world,—all in the Universe is but an expression of this great force, and if this spirit force were not material, were not a substance, how could it take form and have growth in the physical plane? Those still in your world make a great mistake when they for one moment imagine that our world is not a material one; it is foolish to think of an existence without substance. How can there be a world beyond the physical unless it is material? Without it there could be no after-life. Strong invisible bands of force hold the great system of spheres in proper place. It is all mind-force, and all force is life, mighty, unchanging, unyielding, and this mind-power is increased by every individual life that is developed in your creative sphere. It has become a part of the individual life force of the Universe, and each day it adds something to that force called Good. This addition is made, not at dissolution, but from hour to hour, as the mentality increases."

Such teachings appeal to reason, and I accept them. Our earth is still very young; before it took form and shape and a definite place in the procession of world, other planets and solar systems were growing old. It was but yesterday in the calendar of time that the convulsions and eruptions of this earth in its effort to take definite form threw up the mountains, made valleys for the seas, and destroyed in its labour the peopled continent of Atlantis. It was but a little time ago that the pyramids were built and temples were erected upon the banks of the Nile, that Belshazzar in the temple of Babylon saw invisible hands write upon the wall. Grecian and Roman splendour, Mohammedan culture and refinement, Napoleon's conquest, and religious freedom are all things of to-day. Time is no more measured by the calendar than a grain of sand measures the extent of the desert.

There are so many things which we as a people do not know! We have gone into the depths of the earth and learned just a little of geology; we have done something in botany; we have searched the skies, discovered planets, measured distances, and learned just a little about astronomy. We have succeeded in putting a single harness on electricity without knowing what it is, and have developed our individual selves in about the same proportion. But we have really no conception of space or of the thousands of suns and solar systems connected with ours, or of the medium between them.   Science has no conception of the nature and origin of the electric force, and knows absolutely nothing of the magnetic force, the part that it plays in Nature, or the influence it has in this world of ours.   The world has little conception of matter except in its grossest expression.   It knows nothing of solar space.   It has not developed sufficiently to comprehend that the Universe is material, and that the different planes are similar, except in density. The race has not yet developed sufficiently to understand what life is, or the source from whence this atom that develops self has come.   Nor do we yet appreciate or understand the duties and responsibilities that rest upon the individual, and his relation to society and to himself.   Certain elementary propositions have been enunciated and demonstrated, and many so-called great minds say that beyond them we cannot go.   Life force is as much of a mystery to science to-day as it was before the Christian era.

The primary propositions which must be understood are these: the earth is one of many creative planets; progress has only commenced; nothing in this physical world has or will reach perfection; all present knowledge is elementary; there are no limitations; life is eternal and will continue to develop, expand, and increase through the untold ages yet to come beyond man's comprehension of time. Our beginning we cannot know with our present development; knowledge of our end is equally impossible, but the present is ours.

CHAPTER XI

HOW can people be dead and not know it? This was the most difficult proposition that was ever presented to me. All orthodox teaching has been such that it is difficult for any one to comprehend the natural conditions about them. In my first years of this most interesting research, I talked with many who did not know that they had left the earth-life at all. Why did they not know that they had left the physical body?

Let me give a stenographic account of our work on the evening of May 10, 1897, illustrative of the point referred to and reported by Miss Gertrude Spaulding, now secretary to one of the United States senators from Minnesota.

The spirit controlling our work said: "To-night, we must bring into your presence a necessity, bring one who needs help more than you need words of instruction. In this regular work, do not change conditions; if you want to invite strangers, take another night."

A strange spirit voice said:

Q. I am interested to know what you are doing here. I don't want that woman sitting there to take down what I say.

A. She is not here to take down your confession, if you make one. The work we are doing is of sufficient importance to be taken stenographically; that is what the stenographer is here for. Well, sir, how can we serve you?

"I don't want you to call me 'friend,' but as I am here, I will present a business proposition. You like money, don't you? I suppose the rest of you like money too. It does lots of things."

Q. Have you a speculation that you want us to join in?

A. I have a certain block of stock I want to sell.

Q. What kind of stock?

A. Mining stock. It is mining stock.

Q. Is that the most important thing in your mind?

A. That's the most important.

Q. Why do you wish to sell it?

A. I have a good reason, but I don't say very much about it to strangers.

Q.   How did you get it?

A.   Never mind that. I have it and want to sell it.

Q.   How long have you had that stock for sale?

A.   I have had it for about five years. Have not sold it because everybody seems afraid of it.

Q.   Now, hasn't it occurred to you that if you have not sold it, there is something about that stock that isn't right?

A.   I know all about that stock. Are you afraid of it?

Q.   No, I am not afraid of it. You have offered it very cheap, I suppose?

A.   Not so very. I don't believe in cheap stocks.

Q.   You have traveled?

A.   Traveled? Traveled from one end of the earth to the other. I have even been to Europe.

Q.   Now, does it not seem strange to you that you have traveled so far and not sold your stock?

A.   I'll tell you. It is strange to me because everybody that I have offered it to, has turned away after looking at it. People think I am a little "off."

Q.   Now, where is your family?

A.   You want my wife to sign the papers?

Q. Will she sign?

A. It is not necessary.

Q. Where is she?

A. Home.

Q. Where is home?

A. I will tell you, if you want to know. She is at San Jose, California.

Q. You have traveled a good way. Did you ever hear of the city of Buffalo?

A. Yes, who hasn't?

Q. It is a good city, isn't it?

A. Very good, very good.

Q. Now, I live in Buffalo. I am in my own home now.

A. You don't mean to say that I am in Buffalo?

Q. Yes.

A. Your home?

Q. Yes. You have been brought here for some purpose other than selling mining stock. You have traveled a long way. Now, my friend, where did you get those papers? Be honest with me. Have they not been a burden to you for years?

A. That will do, gentlemen.

Q. Did you get that stock honestly?

The voice of the control interrupted, speaking with great force; "The man you stole the papers from, shot you."

Q. Who is that? How does he know? How does he know?

The control speaking to us said:

"He was shot while stealing those papers. When we cannot reach spirits of his kind, we find it necessary to bring them into the conditions prevailing here now; we want your help. In this condition their mental activities are quickened, and they are brought out of mental darkness."

I said to the spirit: "If you will come and touch me, possibly you will gather more strength."

A. You will put handcuffs on me.

Q. You are among friends.

A. I don't trust in friends or strangers.

Q. I want you to listen to what I have to say. You are nearly three thousand miles from San Jose, California. When you were stealing that stock from that other man, you heard the click of a revolver, didn't you?

A. Yes.

Q. Did you hear the explosion?

A. No.

Q. There was one.

A. I should have heard it if there had been.

Q. There was a revolver fired at that time, I am told, and that ball penetrated your body. When that occurred, you passed out of the physical body. You live right on; that life is so like the life here, that you and thousands of others go right on without being conscious of the change; they find conditions so similar, and whatever was in the mind when the change occurred is held sometimes indefinitely. You have been wandering over the face of the earth holding the thought that that stock was in your hands. You are not as you were before you took that stock; a great alteration has taken place, but you are not dead.

A. Am I a ghost?

Q. Let me explain. Every week we sit in a dark room as are now doing, and understanding the laws that govern speech between the spiritual and the physical planes, we are able to talk with people who have passed on, just as we are talking to you to-night. Now, you are in a situation which you fail to comprehend. You must work out of your present condition and undo the wrong that you have done. You will be able in time, much time probably, to progress, and those who have progressed farther and understand your condition, have brought you to-night into this condition for the purpose of having us demonstrate to you the change that has come, and teach you how to compensate for the wrong that you did. If you will listen, you will be told.

A. I believe none of that.

Q. Do you understand that there is actually no death?

A. No, I do not.

Q. The majority of people in the physical world do not understand that change at all. One leaves the old, physical body as one leaves an old coat. But the etheric body, the individual self, with its tendencies and desires, goes on and on. Now, don't you think there has been a change with you in some way? Do you want me to demonstrate that to you?

A. I am just like you.

Q. That cannot be, for your body is composed of ether only. I lift my hand to my face. Can you see my face through my hand?

A. No.

Q. Now, lift up your hand. Don't you see there is a difference?

A. Yes, I can see through my hand.

Q. What do you think of that?

A. If you think I am crazy, I had better go.

Q. We are not trying to do you harm.

A. Talk then in reason.

The control interrupted again, saying:

"We will bring a spirit that shall teach you what is reasonable, and he shall prove to you that you too are a spirit."

Q. Do you know that the man talking to you now, is S——, once a citizen of much prominence?

A. He is dead.

Q. He is talking to you. Is he dead if he can talk?

A. You are a queer lot of people.

Q. Possibly, but if you will listen to what he says, if you will earnestly seek the truth, you will find it. Things are not satisfactory with you, are they?

A. Not very.

Q. Now, you would like to get out of your present condition, would you not?

A. I don't like to be called dead.

Q. We will help you all we can. We want you to listen. I tell you again, there is no death.

A. But you said I was a spirit.

Q. Yes, I say that you are now in the afterlife, and that you have an etheric body, almost identical with the old physical.

A. Don't you know that the spirit is nothing but dust?

Q. I do not; on the contrary, it is as material as before dissolution?

A.   Where are your ministers?   Why don't they so teach if it is a fact.

Q.   Because the great majority don't know; and the few who do know have not the courage.

A.   I will go and ask Father Spencer if this be true.

Q.   Do you want to see Father Spencer right here?   Is it possible at this time to bring Father Spencer here to-night? I asked the control.

A.   I am sending messengers for Father Spencer, who has also passed on since his going, he replied.

Q.   Now, if Father Spencer can come here and talk to you as a spirit—

A.   Then I will believe every word you said.

Q.   Either to night, or at some other time, you shall talk with Father Spencer as you are talking now with us.

A.   I will wait.

Some years elapsed before this strange spirit came again, and then only to say that he had found Father Spencer, and had come to understand the terrible condition which, by a life ill-spent, he had made for himself.   He then appreciated that he must meet again every wrong act of his earth-life, live it again and live it right, and by labour make retribution for all the wrong he had done. He further said that no man, if he understood the result of evil or its effect in the after-life, would do wrong.

At the time this work was being carried on, I did not fully appreciate the fact that one could be dead, so-called, and not know it, I had first to learn that there is individual life beyond the grave. Then I was taught:

(a)—That here and now we have spirit bodies composed of etheric material, as much matter as the flesh garment that covers them.

(b)—That dissolution is simply the passing of the etheric out of the physical covering.

(c)—That the after-life is just as tangible and material as this, intense and real beyond comprehension, differing from this life in vibration only.

(d)—That the so-called dead have bodies as real and tangible to them as ours are to us.

(e)—That many of the dead, so-called, move about even among us, little realizing that any change has been made, unless developed spiritually. When I had learned these things, the teachers of the etheric world took up with me the character and conditions surrounding and governing life in the next sphere of development. Then I understood.

CHAPTER XII

THE ancients thought that Ether filled the sky, and was the home of the Gods. It was contended by Aristotle that it extended from the fixed stars down to the moon. Modern science has heretofore contended that all space is filled with a substance having rigidity and elasticity, with a density equal to our atmosphere at a height of about 210 miles—easily displaced by any moving mass—compared to an all-prevailing fluid or derivative of gases through which heat and light are constantly throbbing.

In "Modern views on Electricity," Sir Oliver Lodge, speaking the last word concerning Ether, says:

"It is one continuous substance filling all space; which can vibrate as light, which, under certain unknown conditions, can be modified or analyzed into positive and negative electricity; which can constitute matter; and can transmit, by continuity and not by impact, every action and reaction of which matter is capable. This is the modern view of the Ether and its functions. The most solid substance in the world is not iron, is not lead, is not gold, is not any of the things that impress our sense as extremely dense. The most solid thing in existence is the very thing which for generations has been universally regarded as the lightest, the most imperceptible, the most utterly tenuous and evanescent beyond definition or computation; it is the Ether. The Ether is supposed to permeate everything, to be everywhere, to penetrate all objects, to extend throughout all space. The Earth moves through it; the sun and all the stars have their being and their motion in and through the Ether; it carries light and electricity and all forms of radiation. Nobody has ever seen it, or rendered it evident to touch or to any other sense. It escapes all efforts to feel it, to weigh it, to subject it to any kind of scientific experiment. It plays no part in mechanics. It neither adds to nor takes away from the width or substance of any known substance. We are assured by some of the highest authorities that the ether is millions of times more dense than platinum, one of the most solid metals known."

Surrounding us and filling what we know as space and permeating all things, is that substance

termed Ether.   It is a subtile essence hard to define
that is in the atmosphere we breathe, highly sensitive, through which the light of the sun travels in
undulating waves, but just as much a substance as
the very rocks and stones.   There is a gross Ether
and there is also a refined Ether.   Through the
medium of the grosser Ether we send our ether-
grams, but of the finer, more sensitive ether, we
know but little.

The suggestion that all life has *etheric form* is
entirely new.   Whether we are advanced enough to
appreciate a proposition so beyond our experience,
is a question, but a moment's reflection, and we do
comprehend that all life comes from the invisible,
and ultimately goes back to the invisible.   The unseen then is the real, and the seen, the result of invisible causes.   There is a world within a world,
all contained in this wondrous universe.   We see
and touch only the outer garment of the etheric universe which, temporarily clothed with gross material, is working out its development.   A directive
intelligence has made all Nature's laws, through
which each inhabited planet moves and has its being, has its domain in the invisible.   The invisible
then becomes a legitimate field of inquiry.

I am assured by those versed in the physics of the
after-life, with whom I have speech, that all life,

down to the atom, and beyond, has etheric form; that every atom that makes up the mass of rock; that every molecule of earth that covers the barren stone; that every grain of sand that forms the ocean shore; that every seed, and plant, and shrub, and tree; that every drop of water that flows in creeks, falls as rain, or constitutes the lakes and seas—all have etheric form. The etheric requires for growth a covering of matter lower in vibration than itself, the same as the seed planted in the earth, and in that outer garment it increases and reaches a higher development. No life force can exist in the physical unless it has a garment suitable for that purpose. Dissociate the etheric form from the outer garment, and the individual can no longer remain an inhabitant of this sphere, dissolution has taken place. Could we follow into the conditions beyond we would ultimately find that every star and constellation has etheric as well as physical form, and that they are visible only because they are clothed with gross material, the same as our own planet, for all laws hold continuity throughout the Universe.

It is the etheric body that sees, hears, feels, smells, and tastes, evidenced by the fact that the physical body has none of the five senses when separated from the etheric. The ear, for instance, with its complicated chamber and auditory nerves, really hears through the etheric brain.   Sever the nerves, destroy the tympanum, and you destroy the communication; put any of the very fine mechanism of the auditory chamber out of commission, and you either cannot hear at all, or at best very imperfectly.   Every concussion causes an ever widening circle in the atmosphere, that is, in the ether of the atmosphere, which at last reaches the auditory chamber, communicates with those fine nerves and with the brain.   By that wonderful process we understand the difference between harmony and inharmony, between sweet sounds and discords. Similarly, through a disturbance set up in the ether we understand language.

Horses, cattle and sheep will exist and wax fat on grass and water.   Put them all together in an enclosed field in a tropical country and keep them there indefinitly, what happens?   They feed on identically the same food, and multiply; the flesh covering wastes and is from day to day replaced, a complete change being ultimately brought about. Why do they not inter-breed, why does each hold individual form?   It is solely because each has an invisible form, that is a form composed of matter in a very high state of vibration which holds continuity, having reached the state termed etheric, at which point the life form neither disintegrates nor enters into new combinations. Man differs from the animal only in development. At the moment of conception, he possesses an etheric body, minute and perfect beyond comprehension, and if permitted to inhabit the physical body for the usual period of time, attains a normal growth.

When by heat we break down the outer garment of a lump of coal, when the physical will no longer hold the energy, the life, or the etheric form, the two are dissociated; in other words, the energy or life-form escapes, to pass into some other state; the outer garment, the cinder or ash on the other hand returns from whence it came, ultimately to be taken up by another form of life, until in time it shall have been so refined that it will hold continuity because it has become etheric. And all this to demonstrate that man is a part of one stupendous whole, evolved from the etheric life in the mass, refined to the point where he holds individuality. Death, so-called, is the passing out of the individual spirit or etheric body from the flesh covering. Released from that outer garment it becomes an inhabitant of a plane where all is etheric, but to the etheric sense and touch all things are just as tangible, real, and natural as when in earth life.

It is utterly impossible for a human being to understand the change in which death so-called occurs unless he realizes that every individual possesses a spirit form composed of etheric atoms, just as much matter as the flesh garment that is visible and tangible. Knowing that fact, he can then understand that dissolution is simply the separation of the physical from the etheric body when the former by accident, disease, or age can no longer obey the will of the occupant. When the physical body can no longer do its part, the spirit or etheric body, by a natural law, abandons the flesh garment, and by that act ceases to be an inhabitant of the earth-plane. This is all that occurs at the time of dissolution.

CHAPTER XIII

THE UNKNOWN LAND

INTO the frozen north, into the terrible cold, at the cost of human life many explorers from time to time have gone on voyages of discovery, have braved the crags and climbed mountains of ice, have faced famine and desolation, until at last upon the bleak and barren plane, a man has reached the Pole and stood upon the top of the earth. Not satisfied that one place upon the earth's surface should remain unknown, other explorers equally courageous have faced the storms and cold, have crossed the crevasses, have braved famine, until at last they have found the Southern Pole. Man has gone to the ends of the earth, has sounded the seas, mapped the wilderness, and now all lands are said to have been explored. But no! there is another land, an unknown land, tangible, material, actual, real, and more intense and beautiful than any now known; this is the next field for exploration.

Into that land all the countless dead of all the ages past have gone, all the living and all those who will in the ages yet to come inhabit for a little time this physical world will go. This being a self-evident truth, what more important field of investigation can there be? Compared with it the discovery of the Poles or the opening of the Dark Continent is insignificant.

If there is a tangible and material, yet unknown land beyond the physical, inhabited by people, why has it not already been discovered? The answer is simple. Ignorance and superstition have been barriers more difficult to climb over than mountains of ice and snow, and notwithstanding the millions who have gone into that unknown land, little effort has been made to ascertain anything concerning it. An illustration may help to explain the reason for such indifference. Before language was written and largely before the advent of the printing press, knowledge was transmitted by word of mouth, and legends and traditions were handed down from one generation to another. Some of these were incorporated in books, and on account of being in print they found acceptance as facts. Chief among them were the stories of the creation and of the conditions following dissolution, and men without thinking for themselves or requiring proof, have blindly accepted legends and traditions in place of facts based on laws that appeal to reason. Herein lies, in part, an explanation of the indifference.

When man becomes satisfied that beyond the physical there is another world, inhabited by all the countless so-called dead, where those whom he has loved and lost, live and work, the purse-strings will be loosened, means will be provided, the spirit of exploration will be revived, and others as brave as Columbus, as reckless as Cortez, as heroic as Livingston, as fearless as Perry, will become pioneers in the unmapped wilderness of the Unknown Land. By their discoveries the world will be enriched a thousand times more than by the explorations of the ages past into the waste places of the Poles. But until the public intellect is startled, until the thought of the world is aroused, a few of us unaided must work alone.

In the after-life I have father, mother, brother, and son. Others similarly situated may be satisfied with the orthodox teaching as to where they are and their condition, but I have not been, and I have laboured to know something of their daily life and how and where in the vast Universe they live and work. Much has been written about spirits and spirit-life, of a Heaven and a Hell where the so-called dead exist, but it is so hazy, indefinite, and theoretical that it has not appealed to my reason or satisfied my desire for facts.

Do the dead live in houses? Why not? The plane where they live being material, why should they not build homes, furnish and beautify them? All the material in the universe is not confined to the earthland. Are they clothed? Why not? Their bodies being no less visible than when in the earth-life, they, having suitable material adapted to their necessities, make and clothe their nakedness, for modesty does not cease with dissolution. Do they require food? Why not? Their digestive organs were not destroyed in making the change. True the process is in a great measure refined so that they take the essence instead of the substance, as mortals do. In dissolution, do those addicted to opiates, liquors, or tobacco, lose the desire, is another question. No; in earth life, it was not the flesh tissue that craved opiates, but the nervous system, the etheric body, and there being no change in the etheric body, the craving continues and must ultimately be overcome The physical cannot enter the etheric kingdom of God. Are the so-called dead homeless in going into the next life? A very natural query. Some people I am told have lived such degenerate lives that they find nothing waiting in the great beyond. A home may have been constructed by those who have preceded them, but they may be unable to reach it for years to come.

However, those in the after-life ordinarily work and labour to create a home and make it ready for those whom they love to enter at once when the great change comes, just as preparation is made when the new-born child is expected into this world of men.

I know something of the difficulty of comprehending that the invisible can possibly contain anything real and tangible. We are in the habit of thinking, generally speaking, that nothing outside the visible exists; one has never seen that substance of which life is composed; one has never seen life because such substance is beyond our vision. We ordinarily cannot see the very great or the very small, only matter where movement is between certain fixed points, and we know little of what lies above or below. With the microscope and a drop of water it was first possible to discover minute matter; with the telescope we have discerned millions of stars and constellations, composing the family of the Universe, which move with perfect order and precision. The possibilities have not been exhausted, and all the secrets of the Universe will not be discovered by the inhabitants of this plane of consciousness. All discoveries, and all progress are the result of research for knowledge, and are gained by effort.

When I was first told that those in the after-life were real people and lived in a world as tangible as this, the subject was beyond my mental grasp, for I had been taught that the world of spirit was intangible, and existed in space, with no suggestion that what we call matter existed beyond the visible; and I never could grasp its reality until I was taught that in this, our present plane of existence, we realize matter only in a certain mode of motion when it may be said to have three dimensions— length, breadth, and thickness. If others must undergo the process which I have needed, they should adopt the same method, and not attempt to grasp conditions prevailing in the after-life until by research and deductive reasoning they have come to comprehend matter in its higher and more re- fined forms and in its different modes of motion. After reaching that point they will not find it diffi- cult to appreciate a condition, beyond this crude plane in which people, once inhabitants of this world, live similar lives, with similar environment. Having cast off the slow vibrating flesh garment called the body they find everything as material as before. I am trying to explain this subject in a simple manner, so that any mind capable of reason- ing and thinking may understand. I find it even then difficult, for the proposition is entirely new in physics. When this fact is finally accepted, thinking minds will work it out in detail and present it in a thousand provable ways of which I have not thought, and then people will wonder that the facts were never worked out before. In time all will come to know that this, like all other natural changes, is extremely simple.

Knowledge of the environment of the next plane, and of the conditions there prevailing can only come from those who are there, and it is from such that I have obtained my information. Let those who challenge the statement that I have had speech with the inhabitants of the after-life remember this fact—that on an average of once a week for 20 years, under scientific conditions, I have done that identical thing and have had speech with thousands of different individuals who have proved their identity. Any one who would deny that fact should have had equal experience, in order to be qualified to speak on the subject. So far as I know no man has ever had the opportunity or received the information as to the actual conditions prevailing in the after-life to a greater extent than I have.

It is a fact to be noted, that the information as to the conditions prevailing in the after-life, obtained by all careful psychic researches substantially agrees.

CHAPTER XIV

PERSONAL IDENTITY

PERSONAL identity has been the stumbling block of psychic investigators. In my work, on account of the darkness required, I have to depend upon the voice and the information given for proof of identity of the individual. I have had in this regard some very remarkable proofs.

It is only by showing that people in the after-life have material bodies and live under material conditions that we can appreciate how they may speak with direct voice and prove their identity. Assuming that they have bodies, that they retain the same etheric form that was clothed with the flesh garment, and that they live in a material world, we do not find the fact that they speak to us and communicate with us in various ways startling; on the contrary, it is reasonable and natural not only that they should do so, but that they should be just as anxious to communicate with us as we are to communicate with them.

I recall an incident that will appeal to the purely materialistic. I was one of my father's executors, and after his dissolution and the settlement of his estate, speaking to me from the next plane, he told me one night that I had overlooked an item that he wanted to mention to me.

I replied: "Your mind was ever centered on the accumulation of money. Why take up the time that is so limited with the discussion of your estate. It has already been divided."

"Yes," he answered, "I know that, but I worked too hard for my money to have it lost, and there is an asset remaining that you have not discovered."

"Well," I said, "if that be true, tell me about it."

He answered.—"Some years before I left, I loaned a small sum of money to Susan Stone, who resided in Pennsylvania, and I took from her a promissory note upon which under the laws of that State I was entitled to enter a judgment at once without suit. I was somewhat anxious about the loan; so before its maturity, I took the note and filed it with the prothonotary at Erie, Pennsylvania, and he entered judgment, which became a lien on her property. In my books of account there was no reference to that note or judgment. If you will go to the prothonotary's office in Erie, you will find the judgment on record, and I want you to collect it. There are many things that you don't know about, and this is one of them."

I was much surprised at the information thus received and naturally sent for a transcript of that judgment. I found it entered October 21, 1896, and with that evidence of the indebtedness I collected from the judgment debtor $70 with interest. I question if any one knew of that transaction besides the makers of the note, and the prothonotary at Erie. Certainly I did not know about it. I had no reason to suspect it. The psychic present at that interview could not have known about the matter, and I certainly collected the money. My father's voice was clearly recognizable on that occasion, as it has been on hundreds of others, and I cite this instance for the benefit of those who measure everything from a monetary standpoint.

Dr. Isaac J. Funk, a man of much learning, spent forty years in psychic research. He published the result of his investigation and many of his conclusions, but he always lived in awe of the criticism of science. I spent many hours with Dr. Funk going over the details of my own work, and I discussed with him many of the problems with which we had to deal. He was much interested in the investigations that I was making with Mrs. French, and for that reason I arranged for her to go to New York where she spent eleven days with him and his associates. There, under conditions that he desired, she demonstrated the work she was doing with me. The result he published in his "Psychic Riddle."

He was always anxious for proof that the voices which he heard were independent, and he wanted evidence of the identity of those with whom I had speech. These points he regarded as important to prove the continuity of life, and in his work he was unable to satisfy himself concerning them. His method was to attempt to prove a fact by the process of elimination, that is, to prove truths by demonstrating their opposite. He, like all other scientific men, attempted to rear a structure by tearing the structure down. This process has impeded the progress of nearly all psychic investigators, and I often said to him that one should seek what he wanted to find with open and receptive mind, always having in his thought that conditions cannot be changed to satisfy any one's particular notion; that we must accept conditions as we find them and make them better, to enable us to gain the end desired. In all of Dr. Funk's published works he left a loophole in his conclusions, that he might avoid criticism should he be found in error.

Some time ago the doctor left his physical body,

and one night soon after, during one of the last sessions I had with Mrs. French, a man's voice spoke my name. The tone was familiar, but I could not associate the voice with any one whom I had known in the earth-life, although I knew a spirit was speaking.

I replied, "Your voice is familiar, but I do not recognize it."

He replied, "I am Dr. Isaac Funk. I have been out of the body but a short time and being interested in your work, I have been permitted to come."

I then said: "You may be Dr. Funk, as you claim, but we cannot permit you to consume our time unless you establish your identity. This is one of the rules that we adopted some time since, for the reason that, knowing the person, we can form some judgment as to the value of what he may say. If you are Dr. Funk and desire to continue this conversation, you must establish that fact."

He quickly responded: "You are entirely right about that; what you ask is fair. I ought to be able to establish my identity."

I said: "Certainly, if you are Dr. Funk you can give us some proof of your identity. During your earth life you always made a great point of establishing identity."

Then he enquired: "How shall it be done?"

I answered: "That is not for me to suggest. You know how technical the body of scientific gentlemen to which you belong always is. If you are going to have a test here, we want it to be evidential. If you are going to prove your identity, you must do it without suggestion from me."

He replied, after a pause: "Identity was what I invariably wanted satisfactorily proved. I recall a conversation I had with you in my private office at which no one was present but ourselves."

"Yes," I suggested, "we had many such interviews."

He then said: "I refer to one at which I asked you to make a special test at one of your meetings with Mrs. French. I asked that when some one with an independent voice was speaking, you put your hand upon the table and have Mrs. French put her mouth upon your hand; you were then to place your free hand over her head, holding it firmly, and in that situation see if you could hear the independent voice. I wanted such evidence to demonstrate that Mrs. French did not do the talking. No one knew of that conversation but ourselves, and that ought to be proof to you that I am Dr. Funk."

I replied: "Yes, I do recall that conversation

at the time and place.   I now recognize your voice, and your proof is satisfactory."

I then put my hand on the table.   Mrs. French at my suggestion put her mouth upon the back of my hand, I put my free hand over the back of her head, holding it firmly, and then I said:

"Is this what you asked me to do?"

Dr. Funk replied: "Yes."

I immediately said: "Dr. Funk, you do the talking, and we will demonstrate that your voice is independent."

Afterward there was a general talk between Dr. Funk, certain of my group of co-workers upon his side of life, and me, and some plain things were said.   I told Dr. Funk that because of his prominence, and as one who had investigated this important subject for many years, he could have been a great force for good; that many people in this world of men were interested in him and his writings and were guided by his conclusions, but that he never published them in full, for which reason his readers could not reach a better conclusion than he did.   I told him that he had failed at the crucial moment, and had nullified the good he could have done.   I added that I regarded this as a great misfortune not only to him, but to the world at large.

He replied: "I realize that now more than ever. It is a fact that I was afraid of the criticism of men of science. I now regret very much that I did not fully publish my conclusions. In my own mind there was no doubt."

A spirit answered and said to him:—

"You were the custodian of much knowledge. Through your investigations you learned many things. By reason of your position you could have done much good. That was your stumbling block, and before you can progress, you must become strong where you were weak."

In my investigations, covering many years, in the room in my own home devoted to such work thousands of men whom I have known personally have talked with me, using their own tongues. I have recognized their voices; they have recalled and related countless facts and incidents of their daily life and have proved beyond question their identity, no less convincing than in the two cases to which I have referred.

Again, I have talked with many whose personal acquaintance I did not enjoy when they were in this life, but through this intercourse I have come to know them well, and admire them much. I have heard on many occasions the speech of Robert G. Ingersoll, which no man could imitate, speech as eloquent as when in his lectures he held great audiences spellbound. Henry Ward Beecher has honoured me with his friendship and delivered many lectures on conditions prevailing beyond the physical. DeWitt Talmage has talked on various occasions of the duties of the ministry, and of the conditions resulting to the individual though teaching things that were unknown. He found that there was no progress possible in the after-life for one occupying the position of spiritual leader when here, until he had searched out in his plane all those who had followed his teaching, and had brought them to the truth; moreover he found that he must stand and wait until the coming of those still in the earth-life in order that his error should be corrected at the earliest possible moment.

To promulgate unknown or impracticable teachings while on this earth-plane is a serious matter, and results in punishment in the after-life.

CHAPTER XV

SPHERES IN THE AFTER-LIFE

EARLY in my research I understood that life continued beyond the grave; that personality was not lost; that when one had compensated for all wrongs and made them right, he would progress; but it has taken many years to reach these advanced spirits, and from them learn just what was beyond the first sphere, where our work had hitherto largely been confined. We have often asked what was beyond, or to what progression led, and have as often been told to have patience, that when we were prepared to receive and to understand, the knowledge would be given.

At last the knowledge that has long been desired has been revealed, and we find that the future life has seven spheres, each containing many planes; they are as follows:

1. Restitution.
2. Preparation.

3. Instruction.
4. Trial and Temptation.
5. Truth.
6. Harmony.
7. Exaltation.

I have written of the conditions in the first sphere as I know them from work done there and general information given me by spirit people; but in taking up the spheres beyond the first, I am now able to give the language of those who live in them and who describe them. One said:

"I know what we all know,—that there are seven spheres. I have just reached the third. Sometimes a spirit can speak from his sphere to the next higher, as you do while in the body, but only in the same way. I mean that there is no mingling together. When a spirit goes from one sphere to another, it is quite unlike dissolution in earth-life. He is warned that the change is near and has time to put his mind into a higher plane of thought so that he will be prepared to meet the new life. He says farewell to all his friends. They join in a general thanksgiving and celebration, all congratulating and helping him on his way by strong uplifting thoughts. When the time comes, he is put quietly to sleep, with the thought dominant in his mind that he is to make the change. When he awakes, he is in his new home in the next higher sphere. He has disappeared from the old. There is no old body to bury and decay. Each change is for a higher and better life, and the home awaiting is more beautiful, as he builds with a surer, wiser hand, or, rather, spirit. His home ceases to be among his former friends when this change comes. Thought has fitted him to progress, and when that thought which held him to the lower plane has ceased, the embodiment of the spirit, which is held together by his thought, is visible no longer.

"Each new change is more difficult to explain to you than the one preceding. It is simply a higher life and a busy one in which to develop ourselves along all lines, especially the ones suitable to the individual's taste. In this way, each spirit becomes better fitted to be a teacher and helper. It is a very active, pleasant life, and sometimes seems like a big university town or country, with busy students hurrying from lecture to lecture and class to class. All are congenial and lighthearted there.

"In the lower sphere one sees much suffering among those still earth-bound. They, too, are busy working out past faults and they are often heavy-hearted. Generally speaking, the first sphere is the one where restitution must be made, and where the final wrenching away from earth conditions takes place. The second is one of instruction, a period of study, during which the spirit gains knowledge of self and natural law. The third is one of teaching those in the lower spheres, as I have said. The fourth sphere is one of trial and temptation. The fifth is truth, where error and falsehood are unknown. In the sixth, all is harmony. In the seventh, the spirits reach the plane of exaltation and become one with the great spirit that rules the universe.

"There are others, more advanced than I, who can better tell you of the spheres beyond. I have not been to the fourth, and only know of it as you do, by the teaching of those who are there. We are told that the spirits in the sphere of exaltation do not even there lose individuality. They are embodied in all the beauty and good of the universe. I do not know that I can make my meaning clear. Although they keep individuality, they permeate the universe. They have become so great and universal, we sometimes think they go beyond and must lose their personality; but we have no definite knowledge, and it is generally accepted they do not. It is difficult to understand or appreciate what this last sphere is, the development is so beyond our comprehension. Those in the second sphere do little, except to fit themselves for a broader and better work. Before reaching this condition they have freed their spirit from the burden of wrong done in the body, repaid every debt due mankind, dispelled the darkness of the first sphere. They work with open eyes and clear spiritual vision, and are at peace with all. This must precede the sphere of study and development. I have classes on purity, beauty, and patience, and there are classes on every conceivable subject,— music, chemistry, everything. They are different from those in earth-life, and one has to adopt different ideas. One of our engineers magnetizes your room each time you hear our voices. It is easier for those who have advanced to higher life to reach us than for us to reach you; there are not so many barriers. Yes, we always have places that resemble homes. Thought is not indefinite, and that makes our homes, and while we keep that thought, our homes are permanent. You ask where is that home located. I would say to you that all that is space is peopled with spirits."

This lecture gave to us the spheres of progression. As you see, we were told not only their names, but something of the occupations that are pursued in the higher life. Not much can be told, I assume, but possibly all that a finite mind can grasp. I believe what I have written, not only because I know the one who talked, but because it appeals to reason, and is in harmony with natural law, as I understand it.

True, it is hard to understand where these spheres are, but there are many things quite as difficult of comprehension. Astronomical instruments have shown that it is ninety-three millions of miles to the sun, but this really conveys nothing to the mind, because one cannot comprehend such a distance. We know that light travels at the rate of one hundred and eighty-six thousand miles a second, but what that rate of speed is we cannot understand, for there is nothing tangible with which to compare it. Our actual knowledge of electricity, of magnetism, or even of gravitation is limited, as are all of Nature's laws. Then, is it strange that one finds difficulty in appreciating what space is and how it is peopled? This thought of ours is even now free and can pass through space, but it goes with closed eyes, hears no sounds, and feels no touch. At dissolution, each sense is quickened, and all life that fills space is visible to the spiritual senses and tangible to spiritual touch and brain. Space must then take form, substance, and reality,—in a world of thought, boundless and endless.

One in the after-life gave me a description of the spirit home of a great, splendid mother, built by the labour of love and ceaseless charity,—in the physical as well as in the spirit plane in which she now resides,—one who worked long and earnestly to make women understand the truth so that they might live nearer to the best in nature. Here is the description as it was given me:

"Before me is the interior of a splendid home, the home made by a spirit, created and builded by the thoughts, acts, and works of one who, thirty-two years ago, lived on the material plane. The room opening before me seems like pure white marble with lofty ceilings; around the four sides runs a broad balcony supported by columns gracefully turned; from a point beyond the centre is a broad stairway curving outward; at its foot, on each side, are niches filled with beautiful statuary. Going up the stairs now, I find each step a different colour, yet all blending into one; on all sides of this upper gallery are windows through which come soft rays of light. Opening off the sides are rooms; and, as I look, a door opens and a beautiful spirit comes out, taking on, as she enters, the old material condition that she may be recognized.

She has reached maturity in years, and has a face of rare gentleness—the beauty of purity,—she smiles as we describe her and her home to you. With her is a daughter just reaching womanhood; one that never lived the earth-life but was prematurely born. These two, drawn by the invisible bond of affection, have builded this home and made it rich with love.

"Passing down the corridor now, the mother's arm about the daughter, they approach the other end of the building and descend a stairway similar to the first, and go out upon a broad terrace, along walks bordered with flowers, into the garden of happiness. Turning now and looking toward a valley, I see many trees heavy with foliage, and through them I behold the waters of a lake, rich as an emerald in colour.

"About the vaulted room which I have described are many others of like material, filled with all that this mother loves. Books that she uses in her work are seen; pictures, created by acts of tenderness, adorn the walls. Musical instruments unlike those of earth await spirit-touch. This is a home where girls, just budding into womanhood, are taught purity—this is a mother's home, and suggests to you the possibility of spiritual surroundings. It was not builded in a day, but is the result of labour in the earth and in spheres of progression, where the surroundings are in harmony with spiritual development; the home of a good woman, builded by helping others."

I said to one of my friends in the after-life, at another time: "Tell me of the homes of spirit people," and, in reply, he said:

"That is a most difficult thing to do, because earth people expect to find everything so different, while, in reality, the homes here are practically the same as in earth-life, except that there is in the advanced spheres no discord, no lack of harmony, nothing but light, beauty, music, laughter, blended with earnest, thoughtful study. I am describing the home of a spirit who has grown to know the life-principle. There are many poor, struggling souls wilfully, or ignorantly, looking down instead of upwards into the great possibility of the future, who are living in squalid huts which their deeds and thoughts in earth-life have made for them. Very few have beautiful homes ready for them when they enter spirit-life, for most people live in such ignorance of natural laws that they find insufficient shelter awaiting them, but the wise ones start to build by perfecting their way of thinking and by undoing wrongs on earth, and also, by helping others. No actual physical touch is given these homes, but, as the soul grows in beauty of thought and deed, the home grows to perfection."

"Are these homes as real to you as ours are to us?" I asked.

"They are the abiding places of spirits who gather into them the objects of beauty they love, and there harmonious spirits come and go, as in earth-life. They are as real to them as yours are to you. But we look at things differently; we think them, and the thought is expressed in waves that are visible and real as long as we hold the thought."

CHAPTER XVI

THEIR DAILY LIFE

IN my investigation I was always anxious to obtain a description of the occupation and daily life of those who live in the plane beyond, and asked many practical questions.

"What is this death change that seems so horrible to the average mind?" I inquired.

"Death change," one answered, "is simply the liberation of the spirit form from the physical body, composing the outer flesh garment, perfectly natural and painless. Every change in Nature is beautiful, and dissolution is no exception to the rule. One simply ceases to be an inhabitant of your world, and in an instant one becomes an inhabitant of the world in which we now live. The second world or plane is just as natural to us as the first, but, of course, we live under different conditions. We pass our daily life as before. Our spirit is just as perfect a human form as it ever was. For your clear understanding of the *modus operandi* of the death change to this plane

we may say one parts with the physical body only.
We lose none of our intelligence; neither is anything added to our understanding."

"What of your daily life?" I asked.

"Our days are very busy," he said. "There is
no stagnation, but on the contrary intense activity
among every one, that is, when we have emerged
from the earth conditions. There are countless
millions of children unborn physically who are
plunged into this world of ours, and there are millions of women here who have never known
motherhood in earth life, who take and care for
them, watch and aid their growth, mentally and
physically, and in that manner satisfy the craving
of motherhood.

"The insane pass from the earth-life insane
still, and countless numbers of our people are required to care for them and give them proper
treatment so that their mentality may be restored
to the normal. Murderers at war with humanity,
hanged or electrocuted on the earth-plane, are lib-
erated in this community, and we are obliged to do
what the world of men failed to do—control and
educate them. Then, again, we have the ignorant
and vicious. The atom of Good that has found
expression in them must be developed and directed.
Few people come into this life with any conception

of what or where it is, or of the controlling laws. The ignorance of the masses is pitiful. They enter our portals as helpless as the babe enters yours. So you see dissolution making no mental change, and life being material and continuous, there is just as great need for schools, colleges, and universities as exists with you. In fact, it may be said that everything you have in your earth life is but a poor imitation of what exists here and is largely the result of spirit influence and power."

"What of your homes?" I asked.

"We have houses in which the family relation is continued, where every member-spirit is seeking enlightenment. The law of attraction is the dominant force here. We have a great number of thoughtful men seeking to discover and develop the hidden forces of Nature; we have great lecture halls where those who are learned discourse upon the hidden forces; we have teachers who develop the spirituality, and discourse upon that great force called Good and its function in the universe. It is a busy world where every one is doing his or her part. We do not have any strife for money or need for money; so you see the occupation of the great majority of your people is gone. It is only by helping others in this life—and this is equally true of the earth-life—that one betters his conditions and enriches himself. This is the law. The only happiness that the inhabitants of earth really get is through being charitable, doing good, and making the world happier. The only wealth that any man carries beyond the grave is what he gives away before he reaches the grave."

"Tell us something of your foods. Do you require nourishment?" I asked.

"Yes," he answered, "but not in the manner or in the way that you do. Our digestive organs continue their functions, and we require food, but we take the essence while you take the substance. You take food day by day in earth life. The substance is absorbed in the physical garment, but it is the essence of the food that nourishes the spirit body from day to day. The substance is no longer necessary, but the essence is necessary just as it was before. So you see there is very little change in physical necessities."

'Tell me of your political economy," I asked.

"There is," Dr. Hossock answered, "no aristocracy in this land of ours, but mind and merit. The law of Nature which is the Supreme Force, called Universal Law, has to be obeyed, in order that each sphere may be reached. Every individual remains upon the plane for which he is fitted, until he subjects his will to the Universal Law. As he progresses, he learns new laws, but they are fundamentally the same, only they grow more intense and vital, until he becomes a part of that law himself.

"The political economy of the spheres has reference only to wealth, which being unbounded and free as air and light, can, of course, be appropriated by each and every member of society, according to his or her capacity of reception, the supply being equal to the demand. Hence it will be seen that we have no occasion for gold and silver which perish with the using; but the currency of moral and intellectual worth, coined in the mint of divine Love, and assayed by the standards of purity and truth, is ncessary for each one."

"Tell me something of your social life," I said.

"With regard to the social constitution of the spheres," he answered, "each is divided into six circles or societies in which congenial people live together agreeably according to the law of attraction. Although the individuals composing such society unite as near as may be in thought, agreeing in the most important moral and intellectual features, yet upon careful analysis we find that the varieties of character in each society are almost without number. They are perfectly analogous to the numerous members of the different societies on the earth-plane. Each group has teachers more advanced than the members of the group, and teachers often come from higher spheres. They impart to us the knowledge that they have acquired in their progression in the different departments of science, which we, in turn, transmit to those below us, just in the same manner as we are transmitting knowledge to you now. Thus, by receiving and teaching, our intellectual faculties are expanded to higher conceptions and more exalted views of Nature's laws. Our scientific researches are extended to all that pertains to Nature, to the wonders of the heavens and of earth and to whatever the mentality is capable of conceiving and comprehending. In this manner we get our progression and enjoyment. The sciences of astronomy and mathematics engage our attention. These subjects are inexhaustible. Chemistry is the most interesting of any of our studies, as it would be to you if you only appreciated the fact that all change in Nature is the result of chemical action."

"You do not mean to say that all of your inhabitants are sufficiently advanced to do that work?"

"No," he answered, "there are millions of inhabitants of this life who are not sufficiently advanced to take any interest in such studies. As we have passed beyond the rudimentary sphere, our intellectual energy is increased, our perception improved, and we can by intuition, as it were, more correctly and rapidly conceive and understand those principles and truths which are the basis of all scientific work.

"In addition to our research we have our diversion from which we obtain great pleasure. We come together in social intercourse, just as you do. Families meet and have reunions, just as you do. Not one particle of love is lost, but rather it is intensified. Everything is intensified to a degree that you cannot imagine. Your pleasure and amusements can in no way compare to those which we are privileged to enjoy."

"What of the religious movement among your people?" I asked.

"In the lowest of the spheres, that is, in the earth-bound spheres sectarian strife and religious movement are just as strenuous among the people as they were before these persons left the physical body. That state of transition is but little removed from the physical, for, while the majority there know they have left the body, others have such an imperfect appreciation of the change, or have led such immoral lives that they are not con-

scious of the fact.   Here the dogmas of orthodoxy
are dominant, and the old religious teachings are
promulgated, and the priesthood still holds power.
One would think that an individual having passed
through the portal called death and finding nothing
as he had been taught, or as he had believed, would
give up the old notions and try to comprehend the
economy of the natural law under which he continued to live; but, strange as it may seem,
many even then cling to the old beliefs as if in
fear, as if to doubt were sacrilege, and in many
ways excuse their failure to find what they expected.   They go into your churches and mingle
with other people, a great invisible host, hear the
same old teachings, say the same creeds and continue in the same mental attitude until some condition is brought about them that guides them into
the avenue of knowledge, and as time goes on, one
by one they break the shackles about their mentalities, and by progression, through individual effort, become inhabitants of the first spirit sphere.

"Everyday matters are no different in our sphere
than in your sphere.   You do not progress and obtain knowledge and advancement until you break
away from the old beliefs and creeds.   Neither
do those out of the body in that earth-bound condition.   You see there is but one law for you and

one law for us. All of nature's laws are universal.

"Our laws are meted out on a scale of exact justice. All Nature's laws are exact laws, and from their award there is no appeal. Punishments are but the natural consequences of violated laws, and are invariably commensurate with the offence, and have reference to the reformation of the offender as well as to the prevention of future crimes."

"What are the best results that will come to mankind through communication with your people?" I asked an inhabitant of the after-life. He answered:

"I will briefly call your attention to a few of the most prominent of the beneficial results which will flow from spiritual intercommunion. It will settle the important question, 'If a man die, shall he live again?' It will reduce the doctrine of the immortality of the human spirit to certainty, so that the world's knowledge of the fact will not be the result of a blind faith, but a positive philosophy. It will show the relation existing between mind and matter; it will make men thinking and rational beings. It will establish a holy and most delightful intercourse between the inhabitants of the terrestrial world and the departed spirit friends. It will expand and liberalize the mind far beyond your present conceptions. It will fraternize and unite all the members of the human family in an everlasting bond of spiritual union and harmonious brotherhood. It will establish the principle of Love to God and your fellows. It will do away with sectarian bigotry. It will show that many of the so-called religious teachings are but impositions on the credulity of mankind."

"I am always anxious for a further description of yourselves, your pleasures, your intercourse with each other, and it is difficult for us who have only had experience with matter in its physical state in any way to comprehend life in another state," I said.

"We derive much pleasure," was the reply, "from the exercise of our talents in vocal and instrumental music, which far excels the noblest efforts of musical genius on earth. When we convene to worship God in our temples, whose halls and columns beam with inherent light, our voices are blended together in songs of praise and adoration to the Almighty author of our existence.

"We are moral, intellectual, and sensitive creatures. Instead of being, as many of you imagine, mere shadowy and unsubstantial entities, we are possessed of definite, tangible, and exquisitely symmetrical forms, with well rounded and graceful limbs, and yet so light and elastic that we can glide through the atmosphere with almost electrical speed. The forked lightnings may flash, and the thunders roll in awful reverberation along the vault of heaven, and the rain descend in gushing torrents, but we can stand unharmed by your side.

"We are, moreover, endowed with all the beauty, loveliness, and vivacity of youth, and are clothed in flowing vestments of effulgent nature suited to the peculiar degree of refinement of our bodies. Our raiment being composed of phosphorescent principles, we have the power of attracting and absorbing or reflecting the rays evolved, according as our condition is more or less developed. This accounts for our being seen by clairvoyants in different degrees of brightness, from a dusky hue to an intensity brilliant light."

CHAPTER XVII

FACTS WELL TO KNOW

"ARE you ever told by those in the after-life anything you did not previously know?" I am often asked.

Yes, but future events have never been fore-told, for the simple reason that the future is no more known to them than to us. I have been told many things I did not know, and some beyond my comprehension now.

One speaking of the human heart said, "it is the chief organ of the body. It pumps blood every second to the extremities, to the feet as well as to the brain. Every thought breaks down tissues, every movement produces waste. Let it stop for one moment, and dissolution takes place. It is sending life to every part of the body."

"We all know," I replied, "that it takes energy to keep anything in motion, and whenever there is motion there is waste. What then supplies energy that keeps the heart in motion?"

Michael Faraday coming in said:

"You have been told that by the process of decomposition of water you obtain electricity. This proposition you can demonstrate to be a fact. Now oxygen is one form of electricity; hydrogen is another form of electricity called negative electricity; magnetism is in fact negative electricity.

The tremendous power in Nature's compounds called chemical affinity is due to the union or attempt at union of positive and negative electricity concentrated in the atoms composing the different so-called elements of the compound. Chemical affinity is the affinity of electricity and magnetism for each other. Electricity and magnetism are both matter in its simplest yet highest or greatest degree of atomic activity. But beyond the electromagnetic is yet a greater degree of eliminated refined atomic activity which is the realm of spirit.

Electro-magnetism in true equilibrium is etheric, the dwelling place of spirit and the connecting link between spirit and the material compounds in various states of atomic activity. Electricity and magnetism are the male and the female elements in the universe. From the oxygen of the air by pulmonic process the blood gets electricity. From the hydrogen of the water by the digestive process the blood gets magnetism. The oxygen of the water is absorbed by the iron of the blood. By the nitrogen of the air partly mixed with the blood at the lungs, and partly by the nitrogen of the food taken into the stomach, the flesh compound is formed.

Hydrogen and carbon form fatty compounds. One set of blood discs are electric, the other, magnetic. The electric discs have an affinity for the magnetic discs when out of equilibrium. But at the lungs they are in equilibrium and hence repel each other to the left auricle, then into the left ventricle, the valves preventing back-flow; this repulsion of the discs to each other must carry the whole crimson mass forward while the equilibrium is maintained to the capillaries.

The electro-magnetic equilibrium of the two sets of discs is lost in the capillaries and becomes less and less to the right auricle. Of these discs the set nearer the heart because of the inequilibrium, attracts the ones next behind, all the way from the capillaries to the right auricle where, by electric action from the brain in moving the heart to contraction, the equilibrium is again partially established.

Now the two sets of discs repel each other to the lungs and through the pulmonary capillaries where the equilibrium is more perfected so that the repulsion of the discs carries the blood into the left auricle; thence by muscular action into the left ventricle and by further muscular action into the aorta. The heart being in equilibrium to arterial blood and positive to venous, attracts."

The scientists have not yet discovered that electricity and magnetism are the male and female elements in the Universe.

Knowing as I do that everything in the Universe is composed of matter varying in vibration only, and that the spirit-body is composed of ether, electric, and magnetic in its composition, one evening I inquired of one in the plane beyond the physical, one versed in the action of electricity, how it was that electricity could by its action destroy life, and I recall very distinctly his answer.

"You are aware," he said, "of the voltage used in the various prisons when they put a criminal to death. You are also aware that frequently a current with many times the voltage used in electrocution passes through a body without serious injury. It may startle you to know that any person who has been electrocuted, or who has suffered a lightning shock, or who by accident has received a charge of electricity that has apparently produced death, could be restored to life by proper treatment. The charge of electricity, as applied in our prisons, paralyzes the heart action, all the bodily functions, and the person is apparently dead.   But you have probably observed that whenever and wherever a person is put to death under sentence of the law, a post-mortem follows. Death was and is produced by the post-mortem and not by the electric shock.   In the beginning surgeons were anxious to note the effect of the force, and undoubtedly made very careful post-mortems. You would be astounded to know as we know, that post-mortems have lost interest and that frequently they now consist of jabbing a knife into the apparently dead body and passing it on for burial.

When a person receives an excessive charge of electricity, either by accident or design, and the bodily functions are thereby temporarily paralyzed, if the body were immediately stripped, laid upon the fresh earth and sprayed with water, the electricity would be drawn therefrom, and would pass into the earth.   If then artificial movement of the arms and stimulants were resorted to, the heart action would be resumed, and one apparently dead would get up and walk away.   Persons die from electric shock because they are not properly treated.   When the bodily functions are paralyzed and the electricity is not immediately drawn from the body and the action of the heart is not started by artificial means, death will, of course, ensue in a short time.   If the treatment described is administered in time, there is no occasion for dissolution from electric shock. Electricity is life, and life will not destroy life. In this day, where electricity is in such common use, countless lives could be saved if the facts that I am now giving you were known and the treatment applied."

I received this information some years ago and thereafter arranged with one of the wardens of a prison in New Jersey to undertake to resuscitate a convict who was to be electrocuted, but the plan came to the attention of the authorities and was forbidden upon the ground that it was interfering with the due execution of the law.

Society must of course have protection from the acts of the vicious, and laws are properly made to imprison those who cannot be controlled, but the representatives of the people assembled in the various legislatures have not the right to prescribe the penalty of death. There is a limit to their sovereignty. What right have we as a people to electrocute one who has committed murder? The life of every individual comes from God and though it may have strayed far from the path of rectitude, yet the people have no more right to take that life than the murderer has to take the life of the murdered. What right have we as a people to electrocute a depraved criminal and by so doing liberate him in another sphere where he may continue wrong-doing? If the public understood what dissolution leads to, they would stand aghast and horrified at the mere suggestion of electrocution.

Again I am asked, "Do you get teachings from the invisible world that are worth while?" Let me answer by giving just a few among thousands received:

"Immortality is the first promise of which man is conscious; but, as he acquires that which he considers worldly knowledge, he tries to rid himself of this promise. It stays with him, however, and, no matter how often he may deny the fact, his everyday life keeps before him the claims of immortality. The fields, the fireside, the love, and companionship of his fellow beings all suggest Immortality. The very thought that death ends all, causes him to shudder. Life would, indeed, be a hollow mockery if the earth-life, with its joys and sorrows, its lights and shadows, were the end. Every heart-throb is a protest against such thought. Nature not only promises eternal life, but fulfils that promise, else we would not be here to-night encouraging you to better efforts."

"Ages were required to develop men so they could discuss rather than fight over the matters concerning which they differ, and adjust them in the forum instead of on the battlefield."

"If you live a good life, the day of your death will be a great day; for, it will be a day of liberty; but, if you do not live as you should, the day of death will find you in bondage, bound by fetters of your own making. The manacles of earth are not nearly so binding as these will be. Follow where the light of spiritual guidance beckons, and do the things you find to do, upon the way. Many tasks will be disagreeable and not to your liking, but they will be the very tasks you will need to perform."

"I feel that it is my duty to help those who try to help themselves. There are many on the spirit side of life who are so densely ignorant that they have no ambition to become better. They continue on in the same old rut in which they were when on earth. Such spirits are of no benefit to the people on earth as they cannot bring useful knowledge to them. If you were able to see and know the conditions of the spirits in the lower spheres and could contrast their condition with that of spirits in the higher spheres, you would understand how important it is that people should be enlightened upon this subject while they are still upon earth."

"Friends, there is one God, the God of Nature; or rather, the God Nature. This God permeates everything and has absolute dominion over all that exists. You are all children of this one God under whose dominion you are here; and you are here, because you could not help yourselves. You had no say as to that part of your destiny; and you will leave the earth-life under the same dominion —Nature—and you cannot change the destiny Nature has marked out for you. Nature's mode of reform is development."

"What is the use of pictures to a person who cannot śee, or of descriptions to those who cannot understand? The description of the higher spiritual spheres, even if it were given by one of the highest spirits, would be unintelligible to mortal mind."

"It affords me pleasure and joy unspeakable to know that I am still a man and can disclose in my weak way to some on earth the great fact that life continues, and that mere theories cannot stand out successfully against eternal fact. I was ignorant and weak when I came into this unknown country, and was not prepared to advance, until I had learned here what I should have known before."

"What you have gained, what you need will be yours in the spirit spheres. There is the closest love and quickest sympathy between the earth-plane and the spirit world, but we cannot make you understand what our lives really are, without becoming exact counterparts of each other.   You will each find a different home, suited to you and your work.   Your sphere now lies upon the earth-plane, and it is for you to perform the duties allotted to you.   You may not be able to give the ignorant learning or the hungry food, but you can inspire their spirits to nobler and better deeds, while some one else, who is able, provides food and shelter. Let them feel that they have your love and sympathy and let them see that, even if the clouds of adversity hang low, your soul is able to ascend to higher spheres.   It is good to know that you do not travel the stony path of life alone; to feel that, no matter how rough or dark the way may grow, you can, if you will, stretch forth your hand and feel an answering clasp—a clasp that makes your heart grow braver.   The Creator seems so far away to most that, unless they can have the love and help of each other, they feel deserted.   It will always be impossible for the finite to grasp the infinite.   There are thousands who walk secure in the consciousness of 'leaning on the strong arm of the Lord' when, in reality, they are cheered and guided by some unseen friend.   It is this spirit that gives to them the feeling of sympathy and strength that so ably assists them through life. The inhabitants of the spirit world are not bound by dogmas or creeds,—that is, those who have been there long enough to get rid of their earth ideas; and they go forth to do good wherever they find opportunity. The main thing is to be honest with yourself, and just to others. Your ideas of good to-day may not be the same to-morrow. Therefore, do not attempt to lay down a rule for your friends to follow. Let each be a law unto himself; for each must answer for his own actions and not for the actions of others."

"It is not what a man does that makes him great, but what he is. Action is merely thought dressed in visible garb. Being must ever precede doing."

In this manner I answer the two questions so often propounded.

CHAPTER XVIII

FROM DEATH'S SLEEP

"BY what right do you presume to compel my presence in this house?" The room was in absolute darkness; the voice of one called by the world, "dead," trembling with anger broke upon the stillness of the night.

"Do you understand the situation in which you find yourself?" I asked.

"I do not, and will not allow any man to dictate to me," he replied.

"You are not afraid?" I said.

"Afraid! I am not afraid of God or man, and I will not remain here."

"It might be to your advantage if you would," I answered. "I did not force you to come. You are as much a stranger to me as I am to you."

"Who did force me to come?" he asked.

"I do not know; tell me about it."

"As it comes to me now," he answered, "an irresistible force seemed to urge me from a dream-like condition. Suddenly I was awake, in your presence, and immediately concluded that in some manner you controlled my conduct. That I cannot permit."

"You are mistaken there, but does it not occur to you that some great good may come of this meeting?" I inquired.

"I cannot in any way understand your suggestion," the stranger said, "or see how any good can come of an enforced conference. If you did not bring me, who did? I had no desire to come, nor do I wish to remain. This house and its surroundings are unfamiliar to me. With your permission, I will retire."

"Before you go," I said, "I should like to have you know something of the work we are doing, which may account for your coming."

"Well, sir, finding myself in this unfamiliar situation I will not be lacking in courtesy," he said.

"For many years," I replied, "I have been engaged in psychical research, with this psychic who sits opposite me, trying to obtain a practical solution of that great physical change called death."

"What has that to do with me? I am not dead nor am I interested in the subject," he answered.

"Wait a moment, please. You will be interested when I tell you that I have discovered something of the daily life and environment of the individual after he has ceased to be an inhabitant of the earth-plane."

"You are entirely mistaken in your statements; there is no survival—no continuity of life. Death is the end."

"Are you sure?"

"Absolutely," he replied.

"Suppose," I answered, "I could prove to you here and now, that death, so-called, is but a physical change, the separation of the life-force from the flesh garment, that substance with which it is clothed during its journey on this plane—suppose I could demonstrate here and now that the individual has a spirit body composed of matter with form, features, and expression during his entire earth-life, and at dissolution simply becomes an inhabitant of the next plane of consciousness with the same spirit body, is in short, the same identical man."

"There is no such thing as life after death," he said.

"I am going to try to explain what life is, before I give you the absolute proof of what I state. Now follow me. At the moment of conception, an Atom of the Universal Force called 'Good' is clothed with substance vibrating more slowly than the life-force clothed. The individual is as perfect at that moment as the giant oak in the heart of the acorn. We cannot see the individual or the oak tree before or after birth and growth. Life-force vibrates so fast that it is not visible to the physical eye, but ultimately we see the outer covering, that substance which makes both possible. This outer garment of the individual is composed largely of water. The physical body of ours changes once in seven years at least, but with such change we retain individuality, form, and feature. How is this done?" I asked.

"I don't know, and I don't care," he answered.

"Follow me a little farther, please. This entity, this life-force, this individuality, this soul, this 'us,' if you like, is composed of matter, differing only from the flesh substance in its vibratory condition. This accounts for its permanency of form, but no physical eye ever saw or ever will see this self, this spirit form, this soul, so-called, unless possessed of the psychic sight with which, speaking generally, few are endowed. Without it one individual can never see the spirit form of another while an inhabitant of this earth. We are conscious only of physical expression, and sound. Now in dissolution from accident or physical weakness, the body covering that is visible to us is no longer fit for habitation; then the separation, dissolution—death so-called—occurs; the individual through a natural process releases itself from the flesh garment, and stands forth the same man or woman as before, though invisible to the inhabitants of earth. They see but the old flesh body that housed the spirit. They could not, as I have said, see the true self before, nor can they see it after dissolution, because of the intensity, because of the rapidity of the vibration of the etheric body, for our eyes are limited as to motion, as well as to distance."

"That is all very well, but what has it to do with me? I am not dead," he answered.

"If you will be patient I will lead up to the personal application. When one has gone through this death change, one of two conditions may follow; we may never for a moment lose consciousness—it is then just good night to the old and good morning to the new environment. This usually follows a respectable life. The man is the same still, nothing subtracted from or added to his personality, and in the mirror of Nature he sees himself with the same outlines, the same expression, the same thoughts, the same attachments, still a material body dissociated from the flesh covering, the same spirit form that has been his during his journey in the world. But he then appreciates that his body is lighter and more transparent than the flesh substance he has been accustomed to look upon, and he does not resist muscular effort as he did in the old covering; then but for the assurance of friends and relatives who assist in the change, as at earth-birth, and explain to the quickening consciousness, many would be afraid. There is this great difference in the two births. When this atom of life-force first becomes individual, an inhabitant of the earth plane, it possesses instinct but no intelligence; it continues to develop, with no knowledge of its previous existence. It could have none, for it came from the mass of universal life forces. The next great change is similar except that the individual retains all previous development; he knows little more of the laws governing, and the means available to aid his progression than an infant.

On the other hand, those who have led unclean earth-lives, who have been selfish, immoral, and have committed crimes against man and Nature, may not soon awaken; if they do, they find themselves in mental darkness, in a prison of their own building, and there they remain until a desire comes from within for better things. Then the way will be shown by spirit people engaged in such

charitable work. At the beginning, each awakening spirit is told that each wrong act done in earth-
life must be lived over, that as he works he will
encounter like conditions under which the wrong
was done, and in the new life he must correct the
error in the old in order to advance. I recall that
an inhabitant of the next plane once said:—

" 'The justice that meets a naked soul on the
threshold of the after-life is terrible in its com-
pleteness.'

"I cannot accept a word you say about a life
after death. There is no other life—there can be
none—a man dies like a dog," said the visitor.

"That is true in a sense," I said, "for the life
force and individuality both go on. You cannot destroy an atom of matter, you will admit;
so if life-force is matter, that cannot be destroyed."

"This is all very strange talk, but why speak
on such a subject to me?   I am not dead; if I were
and there is life beyond the grave, I should not be
here talking to you."

"I have talked just as I am talking to you with
many who have made that change," I said.

"Do you mean to tell me you have talked to
dead people?"

"I did not say that; I said that I had talked to
those who have made the change called death.

There is, in reality, no death; there are no dead."

"Talk sense," he retorted, "we have all seen dead people, have seen their bodies buried, and you tell me there are no dead."

Again I said, "You fail to understand what I have been telling you. We bury the physical bodies but not the spirit bodies; one is just as material as the other."

"I don't comprehend you, and I don't care to continue the discussion. I think I will say good-night."

"Just a moment, and I will demonstrate the fact. Did I not tell you a moment ago that I had talked with many so-called dead?"

"Yes," he answered, "but I did not take what you said seriously; I made up my mind on that subject long ago."

"Now to begin the proof—do you know where you are at this moment?   Tell me if you know."

"I don't seem to know.   This is not my home; the room is strange to me; you are strange too. It is all unreal.   Can you explain the situation in which I find myself?

"Listen to me.   This frail little woman, over eighty years old, who sits opposite me, is the most gifted psychic in the world.   More than twenty years ago it was discovered that under favourable psychic conditions such as prevail to-night we could have speech with spirit people."

"It can't be possible," he said.

"The suggestion," I replied, "is so far beyond the experience of man, that I am not surprised at your inability to comprehend the fact. Wait! Having such means of communication, we have not only learned much of the future state, but, acting in conjunction with a group of people in the next life, we have been able to bring many to a state of consciousness, after the death change, in quasi-material, quasi-spiritual conditions, such as prevail here to-night; and when we are doing work of this character, many out of the body are brought for help by their friends, as you have been, that they may comprehend their situation."

"But I am not one of these; the suggestion is absurd, I tell you. I am as much alive as you, and my body is quite as substantial as yours," he said.

"Hold up your hand as I do mine, and see if there is any difference between the two."

"Yes," he answered, "there is a difference, I now discover. Yours is opaque, but mine is transparent. I can see right through my hand. Is this hypnotic suggestion?"

"No," I said, "you are facing new conditions to-night. Do you know that we sit in intense darkness—and cannot see you, although we hear your voice distinctly?"

"I know," he answered, "that it is not dark, for I can see you, and if I can see you, you can see me; but never mind that; what is the matter with my body? I think now I have been very ill, and one always looks as I do after long sickness," he replied.

"Speaking of illness, what do you recall about your last illness?"

"My memory seems hazy, but it is coming back to me. I recall lying on a bed, the physician waiting, my wife and children sobbing. The doctor said, 'he is passing now.' That did give me a start; there were some who would like to see me dead—but I fooled them—for I did not die. If I had died, how could I be here?"

"What do you know about death?" I said.

"I don't know anything about it, and I don't want to."

"But when that time comes to you, you will be obliged to know, whether you desire to or not," I replied.

"Well, I am willing to wait, and I don't want to talk about it. I never did."

"Suppose I tell you that you have already made that change."

"It would be foolish to tell me such a thing when I am here talking to you."

"Suppose I now prove it to you. Those in spirit life co-operate with me in this work and are often able to bring to the stranger those whom he has known in earth-life, and face to face and voice to voice, the proposition proves itself."

"I tell you," he said, "there are no dead people, and if there were, I don't want to see them."

"You are not afraid?"

"No," he answered, "but I don't want to see them. I have enough trouble with the living without bothering with the dead."

"Is there no one in the next life with whom you would like to talk if you could? Remember that your sickness may have ended in dissolution; your body is different, and you know you find yourself in a strange city."

"Things have changed, but I don't want to see or talk to dead people."

"You find life so material, so like the earth life, that I believe no method but actual experience will convince you that you have left the mortal state, and that lesson must be learned. You have been so intent on our conversation, I think that you have not looked around—look, what do you see?"

"My God! People, people, people! All

strangers, and all looking at me, all with bodies like my own; what strange hallucination is this? Where am I?   What am I?"

"You are no longer an inhabitant of this world but are actually living in the after-life.   Are there none you know among those you see, who, to your knowledge, are counted among the dead, so-called?" I asked.

"Not one, but wait, there comes—John—my old partner.   Why does he, of all men, come?   He is dead.   I helped bury him.   I was his executor. Take him and that woman and the boy away.   I won't see them, I tell you.   They are dead, all dead.   They are coming to arrest me.   How can they, when they are all dead?   Tell me, tell me tell me quick."

"What wrong did you do?" I asked.

"Wrong?   Who said I did them any wrong? I was faithful to the trust."

In answer another spirit spoke.   "No, you were not faithful.   You stole the money entrusted to you for my wife and child, and left them to suf-fer.   There never was, and never can be a secret in the world.   When you kept from my loved ones that which I left for their support and let them die in want, I saw, and all your friends in spirit life saw your act and the working of your mind."

"No secret in the world? My crime known! The dead alive! Have I, too, left my physical body to find life when I thought to find oblivion? Am I to meet all those I have wronged? I cannot face the future! Darkness is gathering! I am falling! God help me!"

The voice faltered, struggled for further speech, and was lost. The gross material that clothed his organs of respiration, disintegrated, and he spoke no more.

We had participated in one of the most remarkable experiences that it has been the privilege of man to have. We had talked with one who had left the physical body, and witnessed his awakening.

CHAPTER XIX

THE IMAGINATION

ABOUT me is the Canadian wilderness, vast and impenetrable. I have come across the American border into the forest as I always do when the days grow long. I am far from the trodden ways of men in a place where one can feel the heart beat of the Universe. In the splendid silence I am able to think deeply and clearly.

The house of logs, surrounded by broad verandas, is built upon a point of land extending some little way into the lake; about the cabin, pines and silver birch trees give grateful shade when the sun is high. To the left are islands covered with hemlock and embracing vines; to the south and across the neck of the deep bay is the rock-bound shore of the mainland; and to the northwest there are woods and ragged rocks, lakes and rivers, and beyond, prairies just as Nature left them before men came out of savagery. The winds, enriched among the trees with those properties that give health, sweep across the point on which the cabin stands on their way down the great valley of the St. Lawrence. Long deep breaths of such pure air fill one's blood with oxygen, purifying it till it grows red, and the nerve fluid ceases to be agitated.

There are voices in these silent places. One may not understand them, but knowing that life whenever found has intelligence, the fact of language must stand admitted. The furtive folk are no less dumb than the deaf-mute; yet who can say that they, denied a speaking tongue, do not communicate by motion with as much freedom as our own deaf-mutes? The ability to communicate each with the other is not denied the insect life or the furtive folk. The wild flowers upon the river bank, the reeds in the marshes, the young trees, children of the parent pine, and the oak and maple rearing their heads into the concave sky must have language or means of communicating with each other; otherwise the scheme of the Universe is a failure. Why should life be created, allowed to develop and progress, and be denied speech? I cannot comprehend life in any form without language. With my conception of life-force the environment is wonderful.

In the stillness of the night, the forest awakes.

The lazy sound of bees, those workers of the day, is no longer heard. The gulls that have sailed through the blue sky from early morn searching for food have gone back into the little lakes, far from the presence of man, and rest on the bosom of the waters with their young. But the workers of the night are awaking; there is a splash, a mink is swimming around the point playing; there is a breaking of branches as the deer come down to drink. I hear a soft foot fall, as the denizens of the forest range for food. Now comes the night song of the whip-poor-will, and I feel in my face the wind made by the black bat's wings. The frogs croak and call to one another from pool and marsh and from the river bank, and then comes the stir among the trees and growing shrubs and embracing vines.

No, I don't understand their speech, nor could I understand the speech of the ancient Chaldeans, but if they talked in my presence I should know it. I know that as the winds sough through trees and vines, swaying the branches and needles of the majestic pines, the sounds produced are as varying as the speech of man.

How beautiful is the morning near to Nature's heart! Every blade of grass that grows in the clearing as well as the undergrowth in the forest is wet with dew and glistens in the sun. All is still, the waters mirror the rocks and trees along the wooded shore, the loon gives a startled cry, goes down into the deep, and sets in motion upon the surface of the waters circles which we are told never cease.

I went by canoe with my guide to explore some distant lakes. We had crossed the divide and fished in waters that had seldom mirrored the face of man, and as we glided along the indented shore, deer feeding in the rushes leaped from the water and disappeared; from the bushes a fox with cunning eyes and upraised foot watched us as we passed; from the deep, the black bass leaped, and down in the clear waters the muskellunge swam lazily over the bars. A dinner on the shore among the sturdy pines and hemlocks, the crackling fire, savory bacon and aromatic coffee to satisfy the appetite, made strong with effort—such was yesterday—and returning home as the sun disappeared in the golden West, having taken a plunge in the waters of the lake, I sat down in a great chair on the veranda to rest. Soon the purple twilight came, and with it the silence like the benediction that falls between toil and sleep, and then the psychic hour when one sends his thoughts out into the great beyond.

I was weary, and musing on the marvellous experiences that had been mine, my thoughts went
out to my own, in the after-life, and to the many
new friends and acquaintances I have made among
such people. There was harmony between the
eye and brain, the tints between earth and sky become neutral. I looked lazily upon the waters,
at the islands and down the long bay, and as I
mused, there fell upon my senses music so distant
as hardly to be perceptible. Was it music at all?
I listened again; it seemed to be in a valley among
the hills. I could not believe my senses; it was
distinct yet not distinct; it sounded like a great
orchestra of string and reed instruments played by
master hands, and with it the gentle wind among
the trees and all the voices of Nature seemed to
blend in one great whole; it approached with soft
cadence and then receded, passing back into the
silence where it was lost.

Looking again, I saw that the harvest moon,
which had just risen over the trees, made a bright
and shining path across the lake, and as I watched
the waters play and sparkle in that light I was
astonished to see a bridge from the farther shore
across the narrow bay leading straight to the point
on which my cabin stood; it was as perfect in outline as the one suspended across Niagara's Gorge,

with the exception that while definite in outline, it was light and almost transparent; the entire structure seemed made of soft, filmy, radiant material, definite yet indefinite. As I watched, I saw some one approaching over the bridge. Soon I beheld the outline of a woman's form, and beside her a young boy, holding her hand. Was this a dream? Startled, I aroused myself, and beads of perspiration came out upon my forehead. I felt the chair and tightened my hold, I looked up and dimly saw the stars and constellations in the sky, and the islands in the lake. I saw again the bridge of light and those who were coming nearer. I shut my eyes, and all the moonlight, the waters, and the islands in the waters were blotted out,— all gone but the bridge of light and those who were upon it.

I was alone in this great forest. Afraid? one asks—yes, at first until I appreciated that I saw not with the physical eye, but through my senses. I was looking into the invisible. I had come to know long ago that the dead so-called were my friends; so there was naught to fear, and I waited for their coming. So distinct was the woman that I saw her dress of white—flowing garments like the Greeks wore in the days of Pericles,—then her face, and as it became visible, I half started to my feet, for it was the smiling face of my mother.   I observed her features—and how her hair fell in folds about her ears; her face was just as in the old days, except that age and the lines of care had disappeared, and as I look she seemed to know that I had recognized her and had noticed the child.   As the two came nearer, a light different from anything I had ever seen shone in the child's face and through his hair; he waved his hand laughing, and still the two came toward me in the path of the moonlight.

I realized that I was having an experience entirely new and that it was important to make my observations with great care.   I took long deep breaths and waited.   My mother and the child reached the point on which the bridge rested and stepped upon the shore, and up the sandy path toward the cabin, so near now that every detail of face and form was visible, and I knew the child was my son, who went out into the after-life in infancy, but who had now grown to about the age of five years.   My pulse was beating fast, as my heart pounded under the excitement.   I was no longer composed, for all my love and longing for my mother and my son swept over me; I started to my feet and down the steps to meet those who came with laughing eyes and smiling lips, my hands outstretched, but as I touched them, they seemed to dissolve and were gone.

I was upon the shore alone; the soft wind stirred the branches. I walked down to the water which was still sparkling in the path of the moonlight, but the bridge was gone, and those who came upon it. This had been no dream, for not for one moment had I slept, nor did sleep come before the dawn crept into the eastern sky.

Experiences little less strange come to others. While Mr. W., we will call him,—one of the most brilliant lawyers in America,—was examining a woman as a witness in the trial of an action some months ago in the Court House in Buffalo, she gasped, fell back in her chair, and was dead. Mr. W., wholly without imagination and painfully material, told me, and I have not the slightest doubt of his veracity, that when he saw his client gasp and fall back in her chair, he rushed toward her, and as he did so, he saw, and plainly saw, a shadow-like substance having the form and outline of the witness emerge from the body and move away. I cite this fact to show that others have had experiences similar to my own, though perhaps not so perfect in detail.

Months have elapsed since I sat upon the veranda about the log cabin in the Canadian wilderness and saw the etheric bridge and two of the inhabitants of the after-life, but the impression— the memory—will never be dimmed in the years to come. To-day it is more distinct than any incident of my life, and now you ask, as I have asked —"What was it?"

At a subsequent time when occasion was presented, I asked a member of our spirit-group to give an explanation of what had occurred. In answer he said:

"I am familiar with the occurrence because I was present. It was an object lesson. We wanted you to see something of the actual conditions prevailing in this after-life, as you call it, so that you could more clearly describe it, and through you, others could obtain some little appreciation of what waits beyond the physical. Before I answer your question in detail, I want to say again, and it cannot be repeated too often, that the body that you see and touch is but the housing, or garment worn by another body, the etheric or spirit body, which is just as much substance as the flesh, but so refined, intense, and so high in vibration that the physical eye cannot see it or the hand feel it. Now in death, so-called, the etheric body leaves the physical housing, ceases to live on the physical plane, and becomes an inhabitant of this plane where everything is etheric, matter simply vibrating more rapidly than such substance as is seen ordinarily by men. We repeat this proposition to you, and you should repeat it to others as often as occasion is presented, because it is entirely new in physics, and so beyond the world's teaching that even with oft-repeated telling it will be found difficult of comprehension. It was with this end in view that great effort was made to give you the demonstration which we did.

"In further answer to your question," said the member of the spirit group, "you must know, that there is no such thing as imagination, as that word is generally used. Your dictionaries define it as 'the image-making power of the mind; the power to create or reproduce ideally an object previously perceived; the power to call up mental images.' There must exist the sun before there can be the shadow, the real must precede the imitation, there must be the original before the copy, the subject before the photograph. One cannot imagine something that has no existence in Nature. The imagination must have something basic. The etheric mental lines or waves of the mind ordinarily move at will in and about the unknown land, and through the sub-conscious brain get impressions and suggestions, usually intangible and indefinite. Such wandering of the mind not being understood, an entirely false conception is obtained of the mental operation. Everything in the Universe is real, is material, and the groping of the mind in the mental plane, is called imagination, the word itself being derived from image, reflection, the likeness of something else. All this leads up to your personal experience. What you saw actually existed, the bridge was real, and the mother and the little son actually crossed, and came to you as you relate.

But you did not see with your physical eye; you were alone in the great forest, and around you all was natural; there was perfect harmony between you and your environment; your thought was passive, and we, coming in close contact with your brain, touched and quickened or rather sensitized your psychic sense, and by that process you saw more surely than would have been possible with the physical eye. It is only on rare occasions that it is given to one without psychic sight fully developed to look into the invisible, and it may never come to you again. The bridge you saw was composed of etheric substance, actual and real, constructed by mental operations, rather than by the hands. The mind can only fashion gross matter into form by use of the hands, but etheric forms may be fashioned and changed by mental operation alone, and those whom you saw were your own; they had bodies, etheric bodies, and they were clothed in etheric garments. As you know, they are not lost, but live and progress in this, the mental sphere, waiting until the period of your development in the physical is completed. Then will come the reunion, the meeting, and, together, life everlasting."

When will the mind grasp the proposition that all natural changes planned by the Master Intelligence mean progress—when shall we as a people be able to look upon the last great change understandingly, when shall we become big enough to think of the opportunity given to the one who goes forth, instead of thinking of our temporary loss? If the world would only comprehend that death means living on in more splendid environment, and that those who have gone forth continue to live in a world no less material than this, the burden of sorrow and the awful fear of what is called death would pass from the human heart. Ignorance is the parent of fear. What matters it whether one goes out this year or next? In the after-life time does not exist, and progress is eternal.

CHAPTER XX

THE inhabitants of this invisible world influence and in some measure control the thought and conduct of every individual. They are more progressive than we, and having no incentive to accumulate money, devote themselves to the acquisition of knowledge. They delve deeply into the forces of Nature, and dealing with matter in greater refinement, make from time to time discoveries, some of which are utilized on the physical plane.

Faraday, who first made practical the force known as electricity, did not cease his investigations with dissolution, but has been a potent factor in its development through suggestion to those who devote their time to the utilization of that force. Raphael did not cease to portray upon canvas his wonderful creations, nor did Michael Angelo lose his ability to chisel marble into forms of beauty when he ceased to inhabit this plane.

The years that have elapsed since they went on, have been years of opportunity and progress. Mozart, Beethoven, and all the other musicians who gave us our great compositions, have they gone down into the silent and relentless darkness, or have they continued their work, impressing on others from day to day new music that enriches the world? Milton, Dryden, Pope, Goldsmith, Moore, Wordsworth, Burns, Browning of modern times, Seneca, Pliny the Elder, Plutarch, Epictetus, Tacitus and Cervantes, of an earlier period, were all their wonderful writings and philosophies produced without suggestion from the master minds in the more advanced spheres? I know this one fact, that people in the after-life are so close, so in touch with our thoughts that it is difficult for any one to say that this or that is the product of his own intellect. Progress owes much to the invisible.

Robert G. Ingersoll, well known to me in the after life, speaking on this subject said:

"Let me give the most remarkable illustration of spirit suggestion—the immortal Shakespeare. Neither of his parents could read or write. He grew up in a small village among ignorant people, on the banks of the Avon. There was nothing in the peaceful, quiet landscape on which he looked, nothing in the low hills, the undulating fields, nothing in the lazy flowing stream to excite the imagination. Nothing in his early life calculated to sow the seeds of the subtlest and sublimest thought. There was nothing in his education or lack of education to account for what he did. It is supposed that he attended school in his home village, but of that there is no proof. He went to London when young, and within a few years became interested in Black Friars Theatre, where he was actor, dramatist, and manager. He was never engaged in a business counted reputable in that day. Socially he occupied a position below servants. The law described him as a " sturdy vagabond." He died at 52.

How such a man could produce the works which he did has been the wonder of all time. Not satisfied that one with such limited advantages could possibly have written the master pieces of literature, it has been by some contended that Bacon was the author of all Shakespeare's comedies and tragedies.

It is a fact to be noted that in none of this man's plays is there any mention of his contemporaries. He made reference to no king, queen, poet, author, sailor, soldier, statesman, or priest of his own period. He lived in an age of great deeds, in the time of religious wars, in the days of the armada, the edict of Nantes, the massacres of St. Bartholomew, the victory of Lepanto, the assassination of Henry III of France, and the execution of Mary Stuart; yet he did not mention a single incident of his day and time.

The brain that conceived "Timon of Athens" was a Greek in the days of Pericles and familiar with the tragedies of that country. The mind that dictated "Julius Cæsar" was an inhabitant of the Eternal City when Cæsar led his legions in the field. The author of "Lear" was a Pagan; of "Romeo and Juliet," an Italian who knew the ecstasies of love. The author of those plays must have been a physician, for he shows a knowledge of medicine and the symptoms of disease; a musician, for in "The Two Gentlemen of Verona" he uses every musical term known to his contemporaries. He was a lawyer, for he was acquainted with the forms and expressions used by that profession. He was a botanist because he named nearly all known plants. He was an astronomer and a naturalist and wrote intelligently upon the stars and natural science. He was a sailor, or he could not have written "The Tempest." He was a savage and trod the forest's silent depths. He knew all crimes, all regrets, all virtues, and their rewards. He knew the unspoken thoughts, desires and ways of beasts. He lived all lives. His brain was a sea on which the waves touch all the shores of experience. He was the wonder of his time and of ours.

Was it possible for any man of his education and experience to conceive the things which he did? All the Shakespearean works were, beyond a doubt, the product of his pen, but the conceptions, the plays, the tragedies were the work of many brains, given Shakespeare by spirit suggestion. He was but the sensitive instrument through which a group of learned and distinguished scholars, inhabitants of many lands when in earth-life, gave to posterity the sublime masterpieces of the Bard of Avon."

The writings of Swedenborg were produced in the same way. Sardeau wrote by spirit suggestion, and as a fact many of the best works of so-called great men have been in part the action of the minds of those beyond our earthly plane, who, working in conjunction with man, do something for the uplift of the human race.

Knowing as I do the potent influence of spirit people upon the world's thought, and how in every way they seek to enlighten us as to the change

called death, I have wondered what spirit impressed this poem on a mortal mind,—

"As the faint dawn crept upwards, grey and dim,
He saw her move across the past to him—

Her eyes as they had looked in long-gone years,
Tender with love, and soft with thoughts of tears,

Her hands, outstretched as if in wonderment,
Nestled in his, and rested there, content."

"Dear wife," he whispered, "what glad dream is
    this?
I feel your clasp—your long-remembered kiss
Touches my lips, as when you used to creep
Into my heart; and yet, this is not sleep—

Is it some vision, that with night will fly?"
"Nay, dear," she answered; "it is really I."

"Dear heart, it is you I know!
But I knew not the dead could meet us so,

Bodied as we are—see, how like we stand!"
"Like," she replied, "in form, and face, and
    hand."

Silent awhile, he held her to his breast
As if afraid to try the further test—

Then, speaking quickly, "Must you go away?"
"Husband," she murmured, "neither night nor
day!"

Close to her then, she drew his head,
Trembling, "I do not understand," he said.

"I thought the spirit world was far apart . . ."
"Nay," she replied, "it is not now, dear heart!

"Quick, hold fast my hand, lean on me . . .
so . . .
Cling to me, dear! . . . 'tis but a step to go!"

The white-faced watchers rose, beside the bed;
"Shut out the day," they sighed, "our friend is
dead."

This is a substantial description of what is
actually occurring from hour to hour. In the
change as the individual catches his breath in the
etheric atmosphere, and his vision is clarified as
a result of throwing off the flesh tissue, he sees
spirit people, "like in form and face and hand,"
so natural, so unlike what one has been led to believe that it is hard to understand. But let us remember that the change is a natural one, that all
Nature's changes are for our good, planned by
the Master Intelligence, in order that our opportunity for development may be increased, and we
may grow more God-like. Knowing this we can

meet the dawn of the new conditions with confidence and courage.

Man is a part of Nature; his intelligence being developed and refined to a greater or less degree, he is an integral portion of that force which we term God. It is not necessary that we bend the knee and worship at any shrine or altar, but knowing that we are part of that intelligent force which holds dominion in Nature, it is incumbent upon us to do no act unworthy of our position, to live where the best thoughts grow, day by day to strive to maintain the integrity and standard set for us, and ultimately to do our utmost to increase that force called good, or God.

In all ages Man has pursued happiness by countless paths and innumerable roads. Some have thought that within the hollow crown that rounds the mortal temples of a king, it kept its seat; some have thought that on the throne it sat and smiled, and have waded through seas of blood to reach it; some have thought that behind the walls of splendour it made its home; others, despairing of finding it there, have pictured a world beyond, where happiness could be found perfect and complete. But let us realize that there is only one royal road which leads to happiness, and that is to practise the plain, old, yet incomparable maxim, "Do unto others as you would have them do unto you." These sacred words uttered in different form six hundred years before the alleged birth of Christ, fell from the lips of the great Confucius, and are to-day found in nearly every sacred volume of the world.

CHAPTER XXI

NEVER A SECRET IN THE WORLD

THERE never has been and never can be a secret in this world. This is an entirely new proposition, which, if understood, would prevent much crime and unhappiness, and would enrich all mankind. There has always been an idea that many things can be done secretly; that, for instance, one can lie, and it will never be known; that one can cheat and defraud another, and not be found out; that a thief can enter a home without detection; that immorality can be carried on without society being the wiser. All these wrongs are being done under the belief that they can be accomplished secretly, and most of them are done in this manner so far as our world is concerned. Mankind has been taught that God sees all and knows all, but men and women do not believe it; otherwise crimes would not be committed, and the moral code would not be violated.

Pride and the speech of people have a great influence on conduct. Now, suppose the thief knew that if he took the property of another, his act would, beyond peradventure, be exposed in the morning paper, and he would be under immediate arrest. With conviction absolutely certain, would he commit the crime?

Suppose the business man, or captain of finance, knew that if he formed unlawful combinations and defrauded the public, he would certainly be imprisoned; suppose men and women knew that violations of the moral code would be known and censured within the hour—would wrong and crime go rampant through the land? Men and women do these acts in the belief that they are discreet enough to so cover them, that they will never be known. Such people have little idea that every act—I will go further—everything is known by those in the after-life who are interested in our welfare. But they are far away one says. No, they touch elbows and walk beside us day by day. One cannot comprehend God as a personality witnessing each act and knowing the individual thought of over 400,000,000 of people, but one can comprehend the fact that the after-life is inhabited by those who have passed through the earth-life, that they improve their condition by helping those in need of assistance, that by their silent suggestion through the sub-conscious brain, they try to aid us, keep in touch with our thought, and are silent witnesses of all the wrong in the physical world.

I do not mean that all the inhabitants of the after-life know each wrong act. What I do mean is that every man, woman, or child has loved ones in the after-life who take a deep interest in his or her welfare, be their position high or low. In other words, the ties of blood, the bonds of love, the interest of friends are not severed by dissolution. As the father, mother, brother, sister, wife, or child, know by experience the awful effect of wrong-doing, and are able to come about us and witness our conduct, note our mental vibrations and so read our thoughts, is it not the most natural thing in the world that they should try to stay our evil acts? If mankind knew this fact—that nothing . is ever really done in secret—would wrong be committed at all?

Men and women are restrained often by pride; they only stray from the path of rectitude when they think that they go in secret. Teach men the truth, and it will help to make the home sacred, to empty the prisons; it will add more than any other one thing to the sum total of human happiness.

Again, the churches teach in substance that though our sins be scarlet, yet we can become as white as snow, and that there is forgiveness for all sin. One sect goes so far as to vest that power in the church. The practical result of such teaching has been—and is—to license wrong and crime.

Men do wrong under the impression that in some way they will escape the just consequences of their wrongful act. I have said before, and I will say again, that the world is not a jumble, but controlled by law; for every effect there is a cause, and that cause is governed by law. Every act produces a result. Every thought being material creates a condition about us, and is retained in one of the sixteen or more million cells of the brain. When, therefore, any one goes out of this life and enters the etheric where everything, the good and bad, is intensified beyond mind-measure, the storehouse of the brain is opened, and he or she is confronted with the record which has been made. Nothing is forgotten; the good get reward, otherwise courage would be lost; punishment for wrong-doing is terrible beyond words. Every one must bear his own burden, must meet again every wrongful act and make in ways that are provided complete restitution. This is very difficult, and the way is very long.

One who believes that the world of men marks the beginning or the end has no more comprehension of the true situation than the mole, following the path which it has made under the dead grass in the meadow-lands, knows of the physical world.

I have been told two most important truths by those who have honoured me by their teaching: that there never has been and never can be a secret in the world: that man has no saviour but himself, and that the wrong which he does, he must undo. Whatever obligations he contracts, he must meet. I have had other teachings that have appealed most strongly to reason. One of these is "do no worry," but fit yourself to meet situations from day to day. The obstacles which we meet are of our own creation, the troubles we have are of our own making. If we possessed all wisdom, we would then be Gods, and not make mistakes. No one is perfect in this world or has reached full development, and until such time every one as a result of lack of wisdom and judgment will continue to make mistakes and create obstacles over which he will stumble. But that is not misfortune; mistakes are necessary, and it is only by creating and overcoming them that we gain wisdom, and know how to avoid the same conditions again. They are the stepping stones to the heights of understanding, and are good for us. Let us meet them cheerfully and appreciate the lesson each teaches. Ordinary errors ought not to cause us anxiety, for it is only through them that we make progress. A just and full appreciation of this fact would take from the mind the useless burden of worry. Calamity is Nature's spur; trials are not only essential, but are disciplinary; misfortune is opportunity.

Other desirable things which I have learned from this unusual source are: "We have no right to burden others with our sorrows"; all Nature is optimistic, all tending toward good; as one thinks, so he is. There are some men so pessimistic that given the choice of two evils, they insist upon taking both; they see no good in anything and are ever looking upon the dark side, anticipating misfortune. The mind is a wonderful force, its influence extending much further than we have any idea of, and one can do very much to make the world happier. On the other hand, one can do much to make others unhappy by throwing upon them one's own mental condition, and many people by force of habit do this, unmindful of the result.

I recall not long ago a morning in the spring-time. The sun was warm, the air balmy, dande-lions bared their velvety bosom to the sky, tulips and daffodils fringed the borders. The lawns were carpeted with green, birds had returned from the south and were building nests and singing. It was a morning when a temperament that could not respond to environment was poor indeed. As I stepped out upon the avenue on my way to my office, I saw a prominent citizen approaching. His head was bent, his eyes were fixed on the stone walk, his mouth was set; dissatisfaction and un-rest showed in his face. The impression, as his mental condition touched my own, was most de-pressing. I knew the man well; involuntarily turning as I met him, I said:—

"Don't take that down into the city to-day."

"Take what?" he answered quickly.

"The countenance you are wearing this morn-ing," I replied.

He looked at me in amazement for a moment and inquired: "What is the matter with it?"

I spoke with kindness, saying: "It is full of discontent, unrest, and worry; you look at war with all mankind. You will make miserable every man, woman, and child who sees you with your present expression."

"Have I made that impression on you?" he asked.

"Yes," I answered.

"I would not like to create that impression," was the reply. "I have never thought that my mental attitude affected those with whom I came in contact. That is a new idea to me."

"Have you observed the morning?" I asked.

"No," he answered, "I have been so engrossed in thought that I have not observed the day."

I then said: "I want you to forget the things you are worrying about. Look up and see how beautiful the world is, and feel what a privilege is ours to be a part of it. Listen to the songs of the robins, watch the blue birds, respond to the flowers, get in harmony with it all, and as we meet those we know greet them cordially, and watch the effect on them and on yourself."

He walked for a little way in silence; the suggestion was working, his jaws were relaxed, the frown had left his face; his eyes had kindled, his lips smiled. With his expression wholly changed, he walked, a different man, and as he met his friends and acquaintances with a cheery "good morning," his joy and happiness radiated. Others caught the charm of his personality, the world was happier, and so was he.

CHAPTER XXII

MENTAL ACTIVITY

THOUGHTS are things. If not things they are nothings, which is tantamount to saying that thought does not exist. If you design a house, your drawing is an image of the thought-house which was in your mind before you made the draft. You see a certain vessel which is used for holding water, and you name the vessel a bucket. The image of that bucket is in your mind, and when you hear the word *bucket,* your mind recognizes the vessel either because you have seen it or heard it described. You use the word *bucket* in the hearing of a thousand people who have seen or known of the same bucket, and every person of that thousand will perceive in his mind the exact image of that bucket. The word *bucket* is not in the image of the object, but when spoken refers the mind of the hearer who has seen it to the image of the bucket as it is indelibly printed on or in his psychic ether. Drawings are things, images are things—emblems of other things. From these

223

drawings, images, and emblems of things the mind constructs the particular thing in psychic ether, and this psychic house, bucket, or other thing, is the thought, and wrought in material form is the shape and counterpart of the spiritual thought.

It is absolutely impossible for the mind to be inactive for one single moment whether in sleep or awake. The matter composing the mind is in a state of constant activity, so intense in its vibratory action that it is impossible for that substance to be inactive for one instant. The brain in which ideas are fashioned is a perfect machine in constant motion. The creations or product emanating from such instrument are never visible unless physically clothed, and only a very few mental conceptions ever find expression in this world of ours. The mental products from millions of minds in active operation vary as do the products that come from the machines in the countless factories. The mental emanations flowing from a brain highly developed appear to spirit people as lines of force extending and undulating from the soul-center, the longer those lines of force, the more active the substance composing them, and the lighter their appearance.

The electric or gas light, as we use that term, is simply burning substance in a high degree of activity, and the greater the activity the more perfect the light. The mental emanations going out from great, generous souls are light. Those from one selfish and cruel are slow in action and necessarily have a dark appearance. It is like comparing the flame of a tallow candle to the incandescent lamp. Thoughts again may emanate from a brain so undeveloped as to give out but little light, in reality casting a shadow in the etheric atmosphere.

There are millions of those lines of force or emanations going out from mentalities continuously, and they make up what has ordinarily been termed the auras of individuals. Much talk of the aura surrounding each individual has been practically meaningless because of the failure to comprehend that mind is matter, and that thoughts have form and substance. Admitting this hypothesis, we can see at once how every individual is surrounded with thought emanations that go out from his mentality as the perfume goes out from the rose. It may be sweet and intoxicating or it may be sickly and offensive. There is scarcely a state in which man finds himself that has not its counterpart in vegetable life. Those emanations or lines of force are perfectly visible to the inhabitants in the after-life who know from actual observation the character as well as the thought of

the individual. We in the physical world, not having eyes developed to catch those emanations, because of their very high potency, know very little
concerning them. If we knew, our knowledge
would revolutionize the conduct of men. But we
feel the effect of those lines of force when we
come in contact with them; instinctively we feel
the personality of others. Thought emanations
from others, both in and out of the physical body,
make an impression upon our sub-conscious brain,
and these with our own suggestions are continually
entering our brain machine, are weighed, are either
rejected or accepted, and are expressed, so that
there is a continual taking in and throwing off in
our mental operations. It is a process as natural
as the heart action and as little understood. Few
people are able to tell the process through which
and by which they reach their conclusions, but
mental lines of force strike our mentality, come in
contact with our own emanations so that unconsciously we receive an impression and arrive at a
conclusion as to the personality of another. The
first impression that we unconsciously get is always
the one which should guide us.

These thought-lines, as I have said, have colour,
depending upon their length, and as there is no
stagnation in Nature their general condition is con-

stantly changing; that is to say, they are progressing toward the light or becoming darker. As the
individual self reaches a high state of spirituality
with good thoughts and aspirations, the graceful
lines of force reach far, the personality is lighted
up, and we feel the presence of a good man or a
good woman. The ignorant who live for self, with
uncontrolled temper and unlicensed passion have
little spiritual development, live in darkness day
by day, and their surroundings are exactly in accord with their mental state, for every man occu-
pies just that position in society which he is qualified to occupy. That must be so, or the law of
cause and effect would be a failure.

So we see that in our daily life we are creating a
condition about us and around us, spiritually as
well as physically. We are making a physical
condition in which we live from day to day and a
spiritual one as well, and into the latter we pass
at the moment of dissolution. When divested of
the flesh garment, we continue in just that mental
state which we have created and from which there
is no escape, until we, by great individual effort,
change our mental state and acquire new and
higher aspirations and thereby create a better environment.

There are some individuals who bring into a

home peace, happiness, and joy. There are other pessimistic individuals who cast a gloom wherever they go. In the presence of the last-named the laughter of children stops. There are individuals whose personality is so offensive that we avoid them whenever possible. The physical outlines, clothing the personality, are indicative also of the true character of the individual. Men living on the earth-plane are, with our present understanding of these things, very apt to be judged according to their outward or physical appearance. In the after-life, divested of the flesh garment, character is apparent to all those with whom intercourse is held, and many will stand before the mirror of Nature in their nakedness; in truth, our personality has always been visible to the inhabitants of the after-life, because they too are living a material existence, and being etheric, all etheric or mental action is visible to them when they come within the zone of our thought action.

The very proper desire of mankind is to enrich itself, but the difficulty is that we have yet to learn of what true riches consist. True, money is necessary during this little journey on earth, but true wealth consists of happiness, and that is found in leading a chaste, upright, just life, in doing something for others, and being true to oneself. Lives of that character grow rich indeed, and they do not have to wait until the after-life to enjoy the wealth so gathered. Upon the other hand, the captain of finance who, with ruthless hands, has taken from others what they have earned and has accumulated a great horde, having no lofty aspirations, goes out into the next world a pauper indeed, for his better self has not been developed, and the lines of force that have emanated from his mentality are short and dark.

Those who pass out having led fairly good lives, find a condition where it is light, a condition of their own making; in the change they seldom lose consciousness, but pass into an environment where to the limit of their capacity, everything is understood, where without the loss of a day they are ready to continue to labour, to comprehend the economy of Nature's law, to better understand their duties and their responsibilities, and to continue a part of the active force. Those who have led narrow and selfish lives find just the condition that they have been from day to day making, and that condition is a grossly material one. If you were to build a house without windows, how could you expect light to penetrate? The position of men in the state referred to is not one to be desired. If the world would only learn that true wealth and happiness are found in doing the best we can under all circumstances, and that wealth righteously gathered is not only enjoyed here, but is taken into the after-life, the ambition and desire of humanity would be changed in an instant. It is a misfortune to have been wrongly educated, and especially to have been taught that money can purchase happiness, or that money is the one goal that all should seek.

A spirit speaking on this general subject has said:

"You all give off an aura, and if you knew the conditions emanating from some people, you would very quickly eject them from your home. In those whose lives are not strictly upright we find the aura very bad, mixed, cloudy, confused. The emanations of people of good health vary in shade from white, pale pink, to rose colour. When the auras approach the dark colours, browns, greys, and blacks, we know that the person is wrong in some way. Now this aura is influenced by passions such as hate, envy, malice, evil speaking, anger, and when one sets out to do an injury to another, let me assure you that he injures himself far more than the other person.

The power of thought for good or ill is demonstrated in various ways. Let a number of persons concentrate an evil thought upon another, and the effect will be found most disastrous. Again, when a band of people concentrate their thought upon one who is ill, they thereby send him vital force and strength and power. The result is restoration to health. This is the basis of the health that comes through Christian Science practice. It is all the result of concentrating the lines of force at a specified point. The result is good or bad depending upon the character of the force that is projected and concentrated at a given point.

I have been told that a clean, highly developed thought goes out into the ether with the appearance of a search light, starting from a central point and radiating through space. Mind is matter, and thoughts are things, and so wonderfully active is the operation, that we are continually forming our mental creations in such refined substance.

With all our development, and it has been great, we are able to hear only a few of the sounds that vibrate in our atmosphere. With all our achievements we are unable to see motion except it be slow in movement and in physical garment.

On this subject one said:—

We can also read the thoughts of another—conditions being favourable—as readily as you can gain a knowledge of the characters of symbols of a language not your own. Thoughts being motions of the mind, assume specific and definite forms, and when distinct in the mind, can be clearly perceived and understood by any spirit who is in sympathy with the mind in which they are generated.

CHAPTER XXIII

PICTURE OF A CHILD

THE orthodox teachings make no attempt to tell us what becomes of children who go out of the earth-plane in infancy. How many millions of mothers have had babies too young for speech, boys and girls just able to talk and walk, sink into a dreamless sleep, and having kissed for the last time the lips of love, have seen the little bodies lowered with tender hands into the grave, and as the earth fell upon the casket have heard from the lips of ignorance "ashes to ashes, and dust to dust." With hearts without hope they have gone back to the house of sorrow, the toys, the little bed, the vacant chair, the ache in the heart, the tears that fall in countless thousands of homes, and the cries that go out in the night to know where in the vast universe the baby is, if it lives at all.

"What becomes of those who go out in infancy," you ask? "Do they develop in mind and body? Shall we know them and meet them again? Will they know us? Is there any one to comfort and care for them, and teach them? Do they miss and seek the mother love?" These and a thousand more questions have been asked in the countless ages that have gone, and are being asked in every desolate home in the world to-day.

Let me tell what I have learned of those conditions through many years of speech with those in the after-life.

I repeat what I have said before and shall say again, for it is the key to comprehension, that the infant at conception possesses an etheric form, at that moment clothed in a physical garment or flesh body. This etheric form is material, composed of matter, and as matter cannot be destroyed; it follows that etheric child-body cannot by any possibility be annihilated.

The infant etheric form by the process of dissolution passes out of the physical garment which it took on at the moment of conception, the same garment that it wore at birth, and becomes an inhabitant of the next plane of consciousness, where all is etheric, where nothing physical can enter. This change may be likened to an earth-birth. There are thousands of childless women, who never in earth-life found expression for the mother-love. These, with countless others who find their greatest happiness in doing good together with those of blood relation, attend at such a time and take and care for the little stranger in the new environment.

Let me give an instance that came under my personal investigation. It is a well known fact that children up to about three years of age are able to, and do see spirit people; some have spirit playmates. The instance I am about to relate was the passing of a little boy, only one week old, who had a sister a little under three years of age, with whom I was privileged to make an experiment. This little girl night after night saw the baby boy, and described him; he was in the same room with two spirit nurses in attendance, while another woman was from time to time described as being present. Again, this three year old sister often saw the spirit-baby when she was away from her home. On various occasions I verified these statements by inquiry from those in the after-life during our investigation, and found that what the little sister related had actually taken place. The woman who appeared from time to time was the grandmother; she, assisted by two nurses, cared for the little stranger, and on several occasions, before he could articulate plainly, prior to his fourth birthday, I heard him speak to me. This was a most valuable experience.

Children in the after-life are cared for very much as they are here. There are those who find their greatest delight in mothering the motherless, and teaching them words of speech and wisdom; so under such unselfish care the children reach mental and bodily maturity just the same as they would if they had remained in this world.

The etheric process of development is interesting; children need mother-love no less in spirit than in earth life, and as the mother sleeps, those in charge place the etheric baby-form close to her heart, where it rests absorbing the love so necessary to its existence. We little know how close the after-life is, how close its inhabitants come to us, the influence they exert on us, or the result of our thought vibrations upon them. Then again, as the children grow, they keep in touch with us from day to day, and when we go out into the after-life, they know and greet us as we enter the life that has no night.

There are in the next life kindergartens, schools, colleges, and universities of learning just as we have here, and what is more, the inhabitants do not cease to study and increase their store of knowledge when they reach a certain age, but there are great lecture halls where the advanced ones teach the supreme laws of Nature, where all are welcome and all go, and so the secrets of the Universe are understood. There is but one aristocracy in the life to come, and that is founded on the refinement and development of character. Measured by this standard, how very poor are our very rich! I have often written that the aristocrats of the after-life have gained their position by helping others less fortunate. They rise by raising others. Those alone stand erect who stoop above the lowly.

Here is what a sojourner in the next plane has said of the little ones:

"Many people have puzzled as to the state and condition of young children in the spirit world, and it is on that subject that I desire to speak, more particularly, to-night. There are millions of young children of all ages passing into the spirit world every year. Some of them are of very tender age, while others know right from wrong. It is an interesting subject to inquire as to what they do in the spirit life. At the outset, I must tell you that there is a divine law in the spirit world, that whosoever passes into that king-dom before he has reached to man's estate upon the earth-plane, shall grow mentally to the stature of a man. You can gather from that that the youngest child, even the infant which has been taken from you, will grow mentally and spiritually on the other side of life. Clairvoyants and others have often described young children in the spirit-life, who have been recognized by mothers and fathers; they perhaps years after, have been somewhat astonished to hear of the child looking much older, and they have not been able to account for it. You will understand that the presentation of the spiritual form is in order that those in the flesh may be able to see them through the physical senses, and to note that they appear to be growing toward manhood and womanhood. I am afraid that many people upon your earth-plane today are neglectful of their responsibilities to their children. If God has given you such a flower as a child, it is incumbent upon you by example and precept to train that child in spiritual things, so that ultimately he will be with you in the kingdom of Heaven and will rejoice in the knowledge that you guided him spiritually when an infant. But how careless are many people with their children! They forget that the child is all the time taking note, not of what they are saying, but of what they are doing. I assure you that if you are unmindful of your responsibilities toward your children, you will undoubtedly have to pay the penalty when you reach the spirit side of life."

Too little attention has been paid to the going out of children; the world has little knowledge on that subject. No greater blessing can come to the fathers and mothers of every nation and tribe than to know that children with bodies too frail to carry them through the earth-life are not lost in going

from among us, but in the other life go right on
with their growth and development under the care
and guidance of good men and women who for love
of humanity do the necessary work, and so enrich
themselves.

I am impressed not to leave this subject without
a word of warning to do no murder. Know that
at the moment of conception out of the mass of the
universal good, out of the life mass, an etheric
atom, a body infinitesimal in size and perfect in
form is clothed, and no matter whether the physical birth is natural or premature, that life-force so
individualized has commenced its journey back to
God, and all the power in all the Universe cannot
change its ultimate destiny.

I am told that into the after-life countless millions of children have come and are coming who
have never had the advantage of a natural physical birth and earth experience so necessary to their
development, but that heartless mothers by abortive
acts and with the aid of dastard physicians have
done and are doing countless murders, more terrible in result than the taking of the life of a
man, because the unborn infant is so weak and
helpless. If this knowledge shall cause any
mother to spare the life of her unborn child, blood
of her blood, and bone of her bone, or the physi-

ician to pause in his criminal act, sorrow untold will pass both by.

Ella Wheeler Wilcox described perhaps better than she knew in her "Ballade of the Unborn Dead" the natural and logical result of child murder

"They walked the valley of the dead,
   Lit by a weird half light,
No sound they made, no word they said,
   And they were pale with fright.
Then suddenly from unseen places came,
Loud laughter, that was like a whip of flame,
They looked, and saw, beyond, above,
   A land where wronged souls wait
Those spirits called to earth by love,
   And driven back by hate.
And each one stood in anguish, dumb and wild,
As she beheld the phantom of her child.
Yea, saw the soul her wish had hurled
   Out into night and death,
Before it reached the Mother world,
   Or drew its natal breath.
And terrified, each hid her face and fled
Beyond the presence of her unborn dead,
And God's Great Angel, who provides
   Souls for our mortal land,
Laughed, with the laughter that derides,
   At that fast fleeing band
Of self-made barren women of the earth.
Hell has no curse that withers like such mirth.

'Oh, Angel, tell us who were they,
  That down below us fared;
Those shapes with faces strained and grey,
  And eyes that stared and stared;
Something there was about them, gave us fear;
Yet are we lonely, now they are not here.'
Thus spake the spectral children; thus
  The Angel made reply:
'They have no part or share with us,
  They were but passers by.'
'But may we pray for them?' the phantoms
      plead;
'Yea, for they need your prayers,' the Angel
      said."

"I want to tell you," a teacher in the after-life
said, "of a little waif that came to us in infancy.
We taught and carefully guarded, and schooled her
in the pure conditions of our sphere until she approached womanhood, but she had no contrasts,
therefore she could not judge of the relative purity
and delights of her environment. In order that she
should be able to enjoy her home and the glories
of our world, it was necessary for her to have a
knowledge of earthly conditions. And so I was
instructed to conduct this child back to earth from
time to time. When this child first returned to
earth and was among your people, she could hardly
endure even to examine the gross conditions, and

could not understand how people could exist in such dark, crude elements.   But, as I led her along from one condition to another, over the road she would have gone had she remained on earth for the ordinary allotted period, I said to her: 'Had you lived your time in the body, you would have been in the condition in which you see these people'   I also told her that they would look gross to her when they reached the spirit state, but that in course of time they would improve enough to assume the state of purity and peace that she enjoyed.   And as we journeyed on, we met one whose earthly experience had unfolded, and the little lady said·   'That one looks different.'   And I told her that this one had received a higher training.   And we passed along to another place in the earth-life where there were children of the poor and ignorant, as well as of the rich and learned. And we tarried until my little charge thoroughly learned the different environments of children on earth, and the great contrast between their homes, daily life, and schooling and those in spirit-life. This child had never known anything but innocence and purity, and she was far removed from the ordinary conditions of the childhood of earth.   It was long before she could, in any degree, recognize it as a reality.

"And, having learned of the methods of training in the institutions of earth, we pursued our investigations farther along; and, finally we came to where there was a great orthodox church; and there, unseen, we mingled with the congregation. She said: 'This churchhouse is not like ours at all. What is taught here?' Presently the services began. I told her to listen attentively to the minister, for here she would get the average experience of the church methods and be able to see wherein a great work, in brave hands, is greatly needed on the spirit side. Then, the minister proceeded with his discourse in his regular methodical manner, telling the people all he thought essential to prepare them to enter higher realms of the spirit. But the girl, now grown to nearly womanhood, could not accept the dicta of the minister, for she had up to now been raised in the spirit world and had learned nothing that was in harmony with methods attempted by the church to enlighten the people and prepare them for future realities. Therefore the teachings of the minister seemed to her so gross, so false, so out of line with all she had ever seen, heard, or read of in the land which had always been her home that she hesitated to remain, but I told her that her future work and welfare required that she learned as much as possible of the earth conditions in which your people live, and the kind of preparation such earth conditions make for their inheritance in our life. But the more the young lady heard of the sermon the more she disbelieved it. In fact, it was so much opposed to what she knew of the conditions on this side, and so different from what preparation while on earth for entrance to and enjoyment of spirit life should consist that at my suggestion she resolved to visit those who had just left the earth-plane, schooled under its teaching, and witness the effect of it; we, therefore, journeyed on."

CHAPTER XXIV

AFTER birth, death is the greatest privilege that comes to mankind. If death did not occur, there would be old age, feebleness, poverty, pain, and suffering forever; with it, splendid life on through the ages, progress, perpetual youth and vigour. Such is the heritage of all who have lived, or who shall live in the ages to come as inhabitants of this plane; such are the benefits coming through dissolution.

"Physically considered, in the final separation of the soul or spirit body from the flesh garment there are no discomforts. As the etheric form goes out through the process called death, pain ceases, and then for a short period comes what is usually called unconsciousness. During the passing of the soul, when the individual leaves the tenement of flesh, when the spirit of man hurries forth from the old housing, there is no sensation. That period of time may be characterized as a sleep; then comes the awakening the return of sensation, consciousness. Such is the true resurrection, and the possibility of that perfect life, unattainable to an inhabitant of earth. After leaving the earth-plane the immortal has been divested of the physical, and progress is unlimited."

Again, it was my privilege to have speech with those living beyond my vision. The room in my house in which I carried on my experimental work was intensely dark; as usual only Mrs. French and I were present. The thought, before so tense, had for a moment become passive; then from out of the silence came the deep-toned voice of him who spoke the above quoted words.

Ever alert to obtain the personal observations of those who have gone on, I said:

"I have been told that the after-life is intensely real and that with you everything is just as tangible as it was when you lived among us. Tell me something of matter surrounding and composing the plane in which you live."

"The most learned scientist," he replied, "among the inhabitants of earth has practically no conception of the properties of matter, the substance that makes up the Universe—visible and invisible. I did not when I lived among you, though I made a special study of the subject. That which you see and touch, making up the physical or tangible, having three dimensions, is the lowest or crudest expression of life force, and notwithstanding my long study of the subject, the idea that the physical had permanent etheric or life-form, that that which you call space was composed of matter filled with intelligent and comprehensive life in higher vibration never occurred to me; so when I became an inhabitant of the plane where I now reside, I was wholly unprepared to grasp or comprehend the material conditions of the environment in which I found myself."

"Tell me," I asked, "of your awakening, and how things appeared to you as consciousness was restored."

"Of course," he replied, "there was the meeting and greeting of my own who came to welcome me, as naturally as one returning after a long journey in the earth-life would be welcomed. Their bodies were not so dense as when they were inhabitants of earth, but they were like my own. Then I was told that my body and the bodies of all those in that life were actually the identical bodies which we had in earth life, divested of the flesh covering. I was also told that that condition is a necessary precedent to entering the higher life, and that such bodies during earth life had continuity and, further, that in leaving the old, I had come into a plane where all was etheric, that is matter vibrating in perfect accord with my spirit or, technically speaking, etheric self. To me everything seemed perfectly natural to sense, sight, and touch."

"Again, let me tell you," he said, "that the outer flesh garment is not sufficiently sensitive to feel; the etheric body alone has sensation. This I have said as leading up to a clear understanding of what I experienced in meeting the new conditions here. I found little body-change—I had sensation and vision—and my personal appearance was in no way changed except that my body was less dense, more transparent as it were, but the outline of my form was definite, my mind clear, the appearance of age gone, and I stood a man in the fullness of my mentality—nothing lost or gained mentally.

What impressed me most after the meeting with my own was the reality and tangibility of everything and every one. All those with whom I came in contact had bodies like my own, and I recognized friends and acquaintances readily. Now I will tell you of the one thing that impressed me most on coming here,—that was that matter in its intense refinement, in its higher vibration, was capable of intelligent thinking and direction. Shape and grasp this proposition if you can; I could not in the beginning—nor could I comprehend at once that all in the Universe was life and nothing else. This fact, which we now know, will overturn all the propositions of science.

In all the orthodox teachings of nearly two thousand years not one law has been given tending to show how it was possible for individual life to hold continuity. Theology has claimed it without explaining how or where. This no longer satisfies the human heart or mind, a fact which accounts for the great unrest among your people in every land. For this reason it has been our aim to explain the law through which life is continued, and so simply to state the facts and explain the conditions that all may understand. The key to comprehension is first to realize that your Earth does not contain all the matter of the Universe, that all that you see and touch is but the substance used by life in growth. When one leaves the earth-condition, divests himself of the physical housing, he, through such change, ceases to be mortal. By becoming a resident of the new sphere he is said to take on immortality, but in reality he has always been immortal."

"You regard the telephone as wonderful," he said, "wireless telegraphy more wonderful still—but we communicate with each other by simple thought projection. You regard the phonograph as a marvellous instrument, but it is crude beside the instruments in use among us. When you appreciate the truth that we live in a state no less material than your own, you will understand that with our greater age and experience we are much in advance of you, and make and use appliances and instruments that could hardly be explained to mortal mind. At some other time I may be permitted to discuss this subject more fully."

CHAPTER XXV

RATIONAL DEDUCTIONS

THERE is not in the universe a single great problem that man can truthfully say he has mastered, that nothing remains to be found out concerning it. The laws that control this world are universal and in force in other spheres as well as in this; they control all solar systems and worlds in space; therefore, a complete comprehension of those laws and their application requires more than mortal life. If this were not so, perfection would be practically immediate and without process, and men would become gods here and now. The most brilliant men who ever lived, knew but little of natural laws and of the origin and destiny of man. Until now little effort has been made to find them out.

The earth is yet so crude, our senses are so dull and our vision so limited, that we fail to realize those emanations and movements of refined matter about us, or the subtle and incessant play of forces around us. From a single ray of light shoot millions of electrons and corpuscles, the basic constituents of matter, smaller than the atom of hydrogen; these, striking blow upon blow, pass by and through us in their incessant warfare with the night, but we feel them not.

We do not realize the quivering and bending of the earth's crust under our feet, caused by changes of temperature or the pressure of atmospheric waves, nor do we hear the fermentations and oxidations of the soil in the changing seasons. We do not even yet know the exact nature of that ether which a recent investigator considers omnipresent and omnipotent. We see the action of gravitation, but know nothing of the medium through which it operates. We hear the wind soughing among the trees; but we do not hear the roar of sap up trunk and branch, the bursting of the buds as they bombard the air, or the speech of growing trees and flowers and grass among themselves; yet life, wherever found, has language.

The vibrations from out the abyss of space would reach our ears if they had more and higher octaves, or if our capacity for catching sound were immeasurably intensified; we do not hear the clang of the planets as they ring down through their orbits, the explosive detonations of the sun, the wild dance and chant of the Nebulae, the comets' note of warning, or the rush of wandering matter of which worlds are made, which must send out impulses and tremblings through the ether to this planet of ours. We are at all times in a great sea of intensely active forces and potentialities governed by a law of which we have little conception.

About us, but invisible to most, a nation, or rather many nations, of spirit-people, "live and move and have their being," more industrious, more active, more intellectual, and more energetic, than we; so intense is their vibration that we do not ordinarily feel their touch, hear their voices, or see their forms; but conditions can be made, and have been made, whereby, notwithstanding our limitations, we may have speech with them, and know at least something of how and where they live, and what they are doing.

There is so much in nature that we do not understand, is it any wonder that, having kept our eyes so close to the ground, we have not discovered this spirit world before? We have made conditions in which it became possible for us to know a little of those other people, and, even though many have not had this evidence, that does not derogate from the truth of the discovery, which must forever stand as another fact added to the sum total of human knowledge. The possibility of communication between mortals and those in the world of spirits, has been proven beyond doubt; and it now remains for men of genius to discover new methods, and to bring into this new field of research, the same intelligent action that is applied to the lower sciences, thereby increasing our knowledge of the spirit as they have of the material world.

Those who, through ignorance or prejudice, decry a new discovery, and so prevent fair consideration, are enemies of civilization. The time has come for man to be free and to think alone. Neither the teachings of the so-called dead, nor the conclusions of the living, can change facts or nullify a single natural law. Truth has neither youth nor age; it is, and ever has been, a brother to reason; it does not need the assistance of fame or science; it has never been in the keeping of any particular class of men; it is the heritage of all who live.

Let this fact sink deep into every human heart: the individual thought must at all times be kept clean and pure, for this wondrous and ever active mind of ours is from day to day throwing the shuttle through the web of life, incessantly weaving the fabric of the condition that will clothe the naked soul on the threshold of the after-life, and those in the great beyond watch beside the loom.

From this great source, I have learned and know that the bridge of death no longer rests upon the clouds of hope, but upon great piers of knowledge, and the heart applauds the brain when one works to increase the force of universal good. Matter is eternal, only form is new, and one who but yesterday in the flush of health faced the storms of life with splendid courage, and whose body lies to-night in the embrace of mother earth, is no exception to the rule. All that was matter, as we use the term, the outer garment, all that gave him physical expression, will mingle with the substance from which it was formed; but his spirit is eternal, his progression will be unbroken, and his horizon will widen as he reaches the sphere beyond. I know that to the limits of that plane in which he lives at first, the human voice will carry, the thought will reach. The so-called dead live here about us, know our sorrows, and grieve with us. They share our happiness, they know our hopes and ambitions, and, by suggestion, through our subconscious brain, they influence our daily conduct. I know that every hope, ambition, and desire of earth is continued beyond this life, as is also the burden of wrong. I know that we are as much spirit now as we ever shall be; that in death, so-called, we simply vacate and discard the gross material that gives us expression in this physical plane. All about this material world of ours, and in it there exists, in fact, the psychic or spiritual universe, more active and real than this, peopled with all the so-called countless dead, who have never died, who, no longer burdened with a physical body, move at will within the boundaries of their sphere, and ours in what appears as space to mortal man.

Their life is an active one. All the new conditions, all the great laws by which they are to be governed, must be learned, and only by individual effort can they live intelligently and well. I know that a wrong act in earth-life must be lived over again in the next, and lived right, before advancement is possible; that the labour is often long, but that families and friends are, in time, reunited and take up the thread where it was broken. I have heard them talk among themselves and to me; many eminent men and women, upon my invitation, have heard the same that I have heard in the material conditions that we have made. I know something of the democracy of death, and that all mankind is beginning to hear and march to the silent music of reason. I know, too, that the highest duty of every one is to contribute what he can to the prosperity of the many; one rich in worldly

goods, may be mentally poor in a land of opportunity, and this individual life of ours, whether it
has had birth within the palace or the hut, no matter how it turns and curves and falls among the
hills as it courses from the mountain-tops, through
valley-lands, lying at times in stagnant pools of
ignorance and vice, festering in the sun, must some
day reach the great ocean of eternal life, from
whence it came, clean and pure. We should ever
look with eager eyes for gems of truth, and what
we find, we should have have the courage to express.

Some mortal lives are so lived that they stand
out like trees aflame along the green and wooded
shore where waters beat with endless wave; others,
like undergrowth within the endless forest, remain
unknown, but each must, according to the immut-
able laws of progression, at some time, obtain perfect development, which is the heritage of all:
this is the law of life.

I know that in the kingdom of the mind there can
be no personal dictation; that there is no God but
universal good; no Saviour but one's self; no trinity
but matter, force, and mind.

I see good in every act of kindness, in all the
words of wisdom that fall from human lips, and to
me all the good in all the world is God.

CHAPTER XXVI

A TRIBUTE

ON June 24, 1912, at her home in Rochester, New York, Emily S. French, the most perfect psychic of modern times, left this world of ours. She had passed on life's highway the stone that marked four score and more, and weary with the burden of good deeds and many years, she crossed the golden bridge from life to life.

On that June day as I stood where all that was mortal of my friend was being put away, memory flashed back to a previous time. I saw the open grave of my mother, I felt again the biting winds, and the chill of another death,—a sensation born of ignorance,—and I recalled my early resolution to solve the problem of dissolution. Again I stood apart, about me hills and valleys crowned and carpeted with green, winding roads, lakes and streams, trees and shrubs and flowers, and when the casket was lowered, the sun's rays, rich and warm, fell upon it, and birds sang merrily in the trees. With joy in our hearts, we among the many who came to bid Mrs. French God-speed, turned homeward, for this good woman—one among millions—had gone to the next life with absolute knowledge of what conditions were to come. She knew that death was not the end, but the open door.

"Glad," one asks, "that she has gone?" Yes, for it is the most glorious privilege possessed by mankind, after a long and eventful career, when the shadows lengthen, to pass to more intense and comprehensive life.

Mrs. French was born possessed, of what Crookes has termed, "Psychic Force"; from infancy she had unusual abilities. She could not remember a time when she was unable to see people and hear voices which were neither seen nor heard by others; for this reason she was in childhood thought peculiar. There came a period in her young womanhood when, with a pencil in each hand, she would write on different subjects simultaneously, easily conversing at the same time. Automatic writing was not then known or understood, and the suggestion that the beyond was inhabited by people, just as this world is, had not dawned upon our mentality. Afterward there came in her presence, under certain conditions, independent voices, that is, a way was found by which the vocal organs of the dead, so-called, could be and were clothed, so that they spoke audibly in our atmosphere, and in this manner came the discovery of another plane inhabited by all the countless dead, where individuality is actually continued—a world as real and tangible as this.

It was my good fortune to meet Mrs. French early, and the compact then formed was faithfully kept to the end. She was as anxious as I was to understand the play of forces in her presence, and without payment she freely gave her time and strength that through her instrumentality good might come, not only to those living here but also to those in the great beyond. The idea of accepting money for such service was abhorrent to her, and she devoted her life to the liberation of the mind, that the mental bonds of superstition might be broken, and that mankind might become better by living more intelligently.

Her work gave the world a new discovery, and her labour opened the door to the Unknown Land. Her love went out to those in sorrow—to the unfortunate, the rich, the poor, and the ignorant, and yet with her great power she was a child, sincere and frank and full of hope as spring, and she ever borrowed sunshine of to-morrow to make the present glad. She saw into the great beyond where the modes of motion were too rapid for physical sight; she knew the needs of others, and her charities encompassed them, and as the years passed, and the results became more apparent, the censure of this little world failed to sting. Her span of earth's life was exceedingly long. For many years her physical ear failed to catch sounds; she grew refined and delicate as her life force ebbed. Some years before her dissolution she became blind, and all the beauty of the physical world was shut out, but still our wonderful work went on. Toward the end she became weary with well-doing, and met the change with confidence and courage.

Mrs. French passed into the next world gladly, for her physic sight had already beheld the glories of her new home; she had more friends there than here, and she had often heard the voices of the husband, who gave his life that the union might be preserved, and of her son who passed just as manhood touched the noon of life. She went not as a stranger into an unknown land, but as one familiar with the way, for just across the border, there waited with outstretched hands and words of welcome countless thousands who had been helped through her effort.

The memory of Emily S. French comes like a benediction. Over every cradle Nature bends

and smiles, and at this second birth it does the
same. She made me her friend by being honest;
I made her my friend by being fair, and so we
worked for twenty years and more to learn how to
expel the fear of death from the human heart.
She grew old as we count time, feeble in body and
blind; yet her courage and devotion never waned,
and at the end she smiled and met the dawn of
everlasting life.

She was an instrument through which a great
group worked. In her presence with the necessary conditions the people in the next plane spoke,
and never again can it be said, "The dead know
not anything."

I cannot give out the knowledge gained through
Mrs. French's instrumentality without paying this
tribute to her. She was the noblest woman I have
known; she was both honest and brave; she enriched herself by aiding others. She helped to
stay the tears that fell from furrowed cheeks and
looked with pity on ignorance and superstition.
She came to know that all wretchedness and pomp
lose distinction in the democracy of death and that
only character survives. To her in the great beyond where she now resides I send my love.—We
shall meet again.

THE END

If "The Dead Have Never Died" has interested you, you should ask your bookseller to
show you the following:

"Four Dimensional Vistas"
By Claude Bragdon

"Creative Involution"
By Cora L. Williams

"God and Mr. Wells"
By William Archer

"The Book of Self"
By James Oppenheim

These are Borzoi Books published by
Alfred A. Knopf, who will be glad to see that
you receive his catalogs regularly if you will
send him your name and address. Write to
THE BORZOI at 220 West Forty-Second
Street, New York.

Made in the USA
Las Vegas, NV
30 September 2021